Hongli Song

The Role of Information Technology in Knowledge Management

Hongli Song

The Role of Information Technology in Knowledge Management

From Enabler to Facilitator

VDM Verlag Dr. Müller

Impressum/Imprint (nur für Deutschland/ only for Germany)
Bibliografische Information der Deutschen Nationalbibliothek: Die Deutsche Nationalbibliothek
verzeichnet diese Publikation in der Deutschen Nationalbibliografie; detaillierte bibliografische
Daten sind im Internet über http://dnb.d-nb.de abrufbar.

Coverbild: www.purestockx.com

Verlag: VDM Verlag Dr. Müller Aktiengesellschaft & Co. KG
Dudweiler Landstr. 99, 66123 Saarbrücken, Deutschland
Telefon +49 681 9100-698, Telefax +49 681 9100-988, Email: info@vdm-verlag.de
Zugl.: Melbourne, RMIT University, Diss., 2007

Herstellung in Deutschland:
Schaltungsdienst Lange o.H.G., Berlin
Books on Demand GmbH, Norderstedt
Reha GmbH, Saarbrücken
Amazon Distribution GmbH, Leipzig
ISBN: 978-3-639-09842-6

Imprint (only for USA, GB)
Bibliographic information published by the Deutsche Nationalbibliothek: The Deutsche
Nationalbibliothek lists this publication in the Deutsche Nationalbibliografie; detailed
bibliographic data are available in the Internet at http://dnb.d-nb.de.

Cover image: www.purestockx.com

Publisher:
VDM Verlag Dr. Müller Aktiengesellschaft & Co. KG
Dudweiler Landstr. 99, 66123 Saarbrücken, Germany
Phone +49 681 9100-698, Fax +49 681 9100-988, Email: info@vdm-publishing.com

Printed in the U.S.A.
Printed in the U.K. by (see last page)
ISBN: 978-3-639-09842-6

Table of Content

Chapter 3   Research Questions and Hypotheses

Chapter 4   Research Methodology

Chapter 5   Research Design and Implementation

Chapter 6   Conversion between Information and Knowledge: An Analysis of the Survey

Chapter 7   Best Practices: An Analysis of Business Cases

Chapter 8   Implementing a KM Project: A Case Study

Chapter 9   A Novel Framework for Effective Knowledge Management

Chapter 10   Conclusion

Abstract

Knowledge has been increasingly recognized to be a primary source of organizational survival and competitiveness, a truly strategic resource. Knowledge management is a systematic process of managing knowledge assets, processes, and environment to facilitate the creation, organization, sharing, utilization, and measurement of knowledge to achieve the strategic aims of an organization.

However, knowledge is an elusive concept. The complex nature of knowledge challenges the knowledge management practitioner in organizations. Different approaches to knowledge management have been attempted in practice, with the technological approach the one most commonly adopted.

ICT offers unprecedented capacities and potentials for knowledge management. The enabling role of ICT in support of knowledge management initiatives is generally accepted by both researchers and practitioners in the arena of knowledge management. However, some researchers and practitioners question the effectiveness of this contribution owing to the well-publicized failure of numerous knowledge management initiatives.

This book focuses on the role of ICT in support of effective knowledge management. Based on a comprehensive literature review, a knowledge management framework was developed for investigating the role of ICT in support of knowledge management. The framework not only centers on the dynamics of knowledge objects and processes, but also focuses on the impact of the internal knowledge management environment where organizational, managerial, structural, cultural and other related elements are intertwined and interplayed.

Based on this research framework, two sets of hypotheses were proposed for testing: (a) whether ICT enables and facilitates conversions between knowledge objects and knowledge management processes, and (b) whether the internal knowledge management environment impacts the effective implementation of knowledge management projects. To test the hypotheses, a combination of qualitative and quantitative research methodologies including theoretical induction, continuous literature review, secondary data analysis, and the conduct of an online questionnaire survey and a case study was adopted in this research.

The empirical findings were drawn from the secondary data analysis, case study and questionnaire survey. A questionnaire survey and a case study were conducted to obtain empirical data for testing and validating research hypotheses. To obtain a better understanding of current knowledge management best practices, secondary data were gathered and analyzed. In order to investigate the conversion processes of knowledge objects, an online survey was used to explore the experience, perceptions and opinions of respondents in the use of electronic resources at an individual level. To identify the factors that can determine success or failure in implementing knowledge management projects, a case study involving the pilot implementation of a knowledge portal was undertaken for collecting and analyzing empirical evidence from the field.

The empirical findings confirm the ICT's enabling role in knowledge management. The results of this research further suggest that the conversion processes between data and information are fully supported by ICT, whereas the conversion processes between data and knowledge, and the conversion processes between information and knowledge are only partially supported by ICT. While knowledge codification and dissemination are increasingly supported by ICT, supportive technology for knowledge generation and application remains much less effective. The critical success factors impacting the implementation of knowledge management projects include organizational, structural, strategical, managerial, and cultural elements. These interlocking elements form the internal knowledge management environment in an organization.

This book provides theoretical contributions by better understanding the nature of knowledge, the relationship between ICT and knowledge management, and the relationship between knowledge management and internal knowledge management environment. It also provides a contribution relevant to practitioners by developing a novel knowledge management framework, which can be used as a guideline of knowledge management efforts.

Chapter 1

Introduction

1.1 Background

Knowledge is commonly referred to as the human ability to effectively use the information available in a specific context for solving specific problems (Alavi and Leidner, 1999; Turban et al., 1999; Davenport and Prusak, 2000; Damm and Schindler, 2002; Jarke, 2002; Tyndale, 2002; Wijetunge, 2002; Zobel, et al., 2004). Information is organized data for specific purposes. Data are raw facts in relation to specific events, business transactions, and daily operations of our society. Data, information, and knowledge are an integral part of our daily lives (Davenport and Prusak, 2000; Hoffer et al, 2000; Damm and Schindler, 2002).

The importance of data, information and knowledge has been recognized for a long time (Bacon, 1759; Alavi and Leidner, 1999; Turban et al., 1999; Davenport and Prusak, 2000; Lehaney et al., 2004; Cepeda, 2006). Bacon (1759) shows this importance in a simple, yet well-known statement, that is, *"Knowledge is power"*. From very early times, sustained succession has been secured by transferring in-depth knowledge from one generation to the next (Wiig, 1997). The study of human knowledge has been a central subject matter of philosophy and epistemology since the ancient Greeks (Nonaka and Takeuchi, 1995; Kakabadse et al., 2003). Knowledge was central to the achievements of the industrial revolution (Wiig, 1997; Cepeda, 2006; Prusak, 2006).

If anything knowledge has become even more important to business today (Wiig, 1997; Davenport and Prusak, 2000; Hoffer et al, 2000; Dalkir, 2005; Prusak, 2006; Cepeda, 2006). The increasingly fierce competition, the impact of globalization, and the rapid advance of technology are leading to the emergence and development of a knowledge-based economy worldwide (Schwartz et al., 1999; Rollo and Clarke, 2001; Romano et al., 2001; Cepeda, 2006; Pearlson and Saunders, 2006; Prusak, 2006). In such an environment, the timely creation and collection of information and knowledge, the adequate storage and maintenance of information and knowledge, and the efficient diffusion and effective use of information and knowledge are of the utmost importance to the sustainability, even survival of modern organizations (OECD, 1996; Drucker, 1997; Alavi, 1999; Bolisani and Scarso, 1999; Zack, 1999; Lehaney et al., 2004; Dalkir, 2005; Cepeda, 2006; Prusak, 2006). It is well recognized that knowledge is the only sure source of lasting competitive advantage for modern organizations (Nonaka, 1991; Drucker, 1994; Wiig, 1997; Boisot, 1998; Lehaney et al., 2004).

The acceptance of the importance of knowledge has now attained the proportions of a paradigm shift whereby knowledge is regarded as central to the performance of modern organizations (Drucker, 1988; Drucker, 1993; Wiig, 1997; Davenport and Prusak, 2000; Hoffer et al, 2000). This shift in management theory and practice reflects the emergence and development of the knowledge era (Nonaka, 1991; Drucker, 1993; Wiig, 1997). In such a scenario, the basic economic resources are no longer the traditional production inputs of land, labor and capital. Instead, knowledge has widely been identified as the prime organizational asset (Drucker, 1993; Wiig, 1997; Kakabadse et al., 2003; Lehaney et al., 2004).

The knowledge assets of modern organizations become the key to success in the new economy (Alavi, 1999; Zack, 1999; Davenport and Prusak, 2000). Having and being able to effectively use these knowledge assets enables modern organizations to maintain and develop sustainable competitive advantages. This is owing to the fact that there are numerous barriers in the process of transferring, replicating, distributing, and sharing organizational knowledge (Boisot, 1998; Alavi, 1999; Lehaney et al., 2004; Cepeda, 2006; Prusak, 2006), thus making such knowledge of strategic significance in the business environment (Kanter, 1999; Kakabadse et al., 2003).

To gain and retain a competitive advantage in the market place, organizations are turning to the practice of knowledge management (Grant, 1991; Drucker, 1993; Wiig, 1997), through which knowledge is identified, created, maintained, and utilized. Knowledge management is a systematic process of managing knowledge assets, processes, and the organizational environment to facilitate the creation, organization, sharing, and utilization of organizational knowledge to achieve the strategic aims of an organization (Davenport, 1997; Wiig, 1997; Detienne and Jackson, 2001; Lehaney et al., 2004).

Knowledge management is of the utmost importance to all kinds of organizations (Davenport, 1997; Wiig, 1997; Detienne and Jackson, 2001; Lehaney et al., 2004). Such importance is clearly demonstrated by the development of knowledge management theories and practices for addressing real world issues and problems (Kakabadse et al., 2003). This growing interest on the part of academics, researchers and practitioners has been reported in the literature on the development of knowledge management theories and their applications for addressing real world problems in business (Malhotra, 2000; Martensson, 2000; Chauvel and Despres, 2002; Schultze and Leidner, 2002; Desouza, 2003; Liao, 2003; Song et al., 2004).

Hibbard (1997), for example, points out that US companies in 1996 paid about US$1.5 billion for implementing various knowledge management projects and initiatives in order to improve organizational performance. An IDC report predicts that business spending on knowledge management could rise from $2.7 billion in 2002 to $4.8 billion in 2007 (Babcock, 2004). Lawton (2001) found that 80 percent of the largest global corporations have knowledge management projects. Smalley-Bowen and Scannell (1999) show that one third of Fortune 1000 companies have included knowledge management initiatives in their strategic planning process.

The advent of the knowledge economy, globalization, the rapid advance of technology, the changing demands of increasingly sophisticated customers, and turbulent competition place increased pressures on organizations (Drucker, 1993; Offsey, 1997; Wiig, 1997; Martensson, 2000; Chauvel and Despres, 2002; Schultze and Leidner, 2002; Desouza, 2003; Liao, 2003; Beccerra-Fernandez et al., 2004; Pearlson and Saunders, 2006). To effectively handle such pressures, organizations have to respond quickly and flexibly to market, serve customers better, and develop new products quicker (Drucker, 1988; Drucker 1997; Teece et al., 1997). To succeed in such activities, organizations need to optimize the value of their knowledge assets through effective management.

The response to the need for knowledge management is manifest across the disciplines and sub-disciplines of management including human resources, organizational behavior, artificial intelligence, knowledge-based systems, software engineering, and business process re-engineering (Chauvel and Despres, 2002; Schultze and Leidner, 2002; Desouza, 2003; Liao, 2003; Dalkir, 2005; Cepeda, 2006; Prusak, 2006). Some of the more specific reasons for this response are depicted in Figure 1.1.

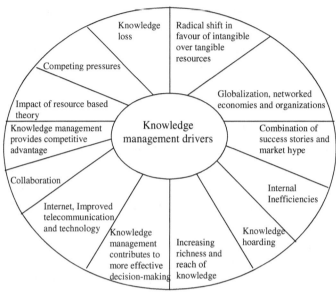

Figure 1.1   The knowledge management drivers

Knowledge management is an effective approach to solving current problems such as competitive pressure (Liao, 2003; Cepeda, 2006; Prusak, 2006) and the need to innovate (Wickramasinghe, 2003). The belief that effective knowledge management can help organizations gain innovation and sustain competitive advantages was enhanced by the success of knowledge management pioneers such as BULABS in the US and Skandia in Sweden (Miller, 1996; Wiig, 1997; Prusak, 2006). Miller (1996) shows that the positive experiences from adopting effective organizational knowledge management in a firm include reduced time to market, improved innovation, and improved personal productivity. At Ford, for example, the development time for designing cars was reduced from 36 to 24 months just by sharing organizational knowledge across the company. Likewise, the delivery delays were reduced from 50 days to 15 days through knowledge sharing with car dealers (Gazeau, 1998). Benefits reported elsewhere include (a) responding to customers quickly, (b) developing new products rapidly, (c) shortening the response time for client engagements, (d) improving project management, (e) increasing staff participation, (f) enhancing communication, (g) making the opinions of operations staff more visible, (h) reducing problem-solving time, (i) better client services, and (j) better measurement and accountability (Nonaka, 1991; Carlsson, 1996; Alavi and Leidner, 1999; Alavi and Leidner, 2001; Chauvel and Despres, 2002).

More generally, knowledge-driven organizations have significantly outperformed their competitors (Nonaka, 1994; Grant, 1996; Spender, 1996), with returns to shareholders for the leading knowledge-driven organizations nearly double that of the median for the Fortune 500 (Teleos, 2004).

Furthermore, there is ample evidence that failure to engage in knowledge management can be a risky business. A survey of European firms (KPMG, 1998) points out that almost half of the companies reported have suffered a significant setback from losing key staff. The results included impaired client or supplier relations and a loss of revenue in some cases because of the departure of a single employee. These departures also resulted in significant loss of knowledge.

Despite the popularity and spread of knowledge management, it remains an elusive concept with numerous definitions, dimensions, perspectives, components and types. To some extent this stems from the complexity and multi-faceted nature of knowledge (Nonaka and Takeuchi, 1995; Davenport and Prusak, 2000; Alavi and Leidner, 2001; Song et al. 2004). Although knowledge has always been important, its significance in a business context developed much more recently (Wiig, 1997; Lehaney et al., 2004; Dalkir, 2005; Hislop, 2005). In the 1950s and 1960s it emerged as a focus within the social sciences and again following the success of Japanese manufacturing in the 1970s. In 1980s, linked to total quality management and business process reengineering, it became a topic of interest across the economics and management spectrum. Resource and knowledge-based theories focused attention on organizational competencies of which knowledge emerged as a leading example. Nonaka and Takeuchi's work (based on Polanyi) widened the focus to include tacit as well as explicit knowledge (Nonaka and Takeuchi, 1995).

Today whereas knowledge is regarded as highly contextual and still therefore, not capable of categorical definition in universal terms, it is accepted that knowledge can be a resource (including a thing and a flow) and that as it is socially-constructed. Differentiation must also be made between knowledge (the entity or thing) and knowing (the process by which knowledge is created) (Polanyi, 1983; Wiig, 1993; Sveiby, 1997; Brown and Duguid, 2000; Firestone and McEcroy, 2003).

Knowledge management is if anything an even more elusive concept. For long regarded as an oxymoron (a contradiction in terms) it has now found an accepted place in both research and practice. However, where and what this is, is once again a matter of context and perception. Depending on perspective, knowledge management can be seen as largely a technological, an organizational or a human phenomenon. In terms of context, it can operate in commercial or in non-commercial (including government) circles, in large organizations and small ones, at the level of the enterprise or in individual departments or even specific processes.

However, differences in perception arise. It is now widely acknowledged that the key to success in knowledge management lies in human and organizational factors, and in structures that facilitate the creation/acquisition, packaging/embodiment, transfer, sharing and use of knowledge. This inevitably involves the nature and mission of the organization, its culture and values, its propensity to learn and to innovate and the strategies it puts in place to support these. Technology, for all its benefits and utility can only ever be an enabler and a supporting element in knowledge management (Lehaney et al., 2004).

Nevertheless, technological approaches to knowledge management still dominate. The leading vendors of commercial knowledge management systems (KMS) are in a market that was worth around $8.5 billion for knowledge management software and services in 2002 (Carnelley et al., 2001). Many knowledge management initiatives rely on information and communication technology (ICT) as an important enabler (Desouza, 2003). Lee and Choi (2003) find that ICT support has a positive impact on the combination of knowledge based on a survey collected from 58 firms. It shows that ICT can provide an edge in harvesting knowledge from existing repositories.

McDermott (1999), however, notes that many companies soon find that leveraging knowledge through the use of ICT is very hard to achieve. The application of technological approaches to knowledge management demonstrates some mixed results. Some of such knowledge management projects have been successful (Davenport et al., 1998; Brown and Duguid, 2000; Rollo and Clarke, 2001; Davenport and Probst, 2002; Baalen et al., 2005; Teo, 2005). Failures, however, are not uncommon (Huber, 2001). Ernst & Young (1997) reported that the failure rate in KMS projects reached 58%. This suggests that confusion still continues to be existent around the role of ICT in knowledge management (Davenport, 1997; Alavi and Leider, 1999; Binney, 2001; Hupic et al, 2002).

Expenditures of software and systems are still growing despite the evidence of failure and continued confusion over the nature of so-called knowledge management technologies and their role. This is not to say that technology is unimportant to knowledge management, rather to emphasize that no technology, however effective, will succeed unless it is appropriate to the needs, processes and structures and culture of the organization involved.

It remains the case that many aspects of the relationship between ICT and knowledge management are poorly understood (Hendriks, 2001). An investigation into the theory and practice of knowledge management suggests that there is a lack of a clear understanding of the relationship between ICT and knowledge management. Such a missing link in the literature may have impeded realization of the potential of ICT in organizational knowledge management practices. This has made it difficult for knowledge management researchers and practitioners to understand the impact of ICT on knowledge management and to make full use of ICT potential in the field of knowledge management in today's dynamic and increasingly competitive environment. As a result, there is a need to investigate the role of ICT in knowledge management, and to identify those factors prohibiting and facilitating the realization of ICT potential in knowledge management in order to achieve effective use of ICT in enabling and supporting knowledge management. This has implications for the development and uptake of technology, and for the wider implementation of knowledge management.

This book addresses this problem by investigating aspects of the relationship between ICT and knowledge management, and in particular those factors that operate either to inhibit or to facilitate realization of the potential contribution of technology to knowledge management. The research questions, together with two sets of hypotheses are listed in the following section.

1.2   Research questions

The primary research questions are 'what role can ICT play in knowledge management' and 'how can ICT be used effectively for knowledge management'. More specifically, this research includes two sets of subsidiary questions from the perspectives of (a) knowledge objects and processes, and (b) knowledge management projects.

Knowledge, information and data are concepts central to the technological dimension of knowledge management. Relationships among data, information and knowledge are commonly the starting point for investigations of the use of ICT in knowledge management (Nonaka and Takeuchi, 1995; Davenport and Prusak, 2000; Alavi and Leidner, 2001; Song et al. 2004). A better understanding of the nature of knowledge and its relationship with data and information, can form a strong basis for further investigation into the role of ICT related to knowledge itself. Following this line of thought, this study defines one set of subsidiary research questions as follows:

- What roles do data and information play in the use of ICT to support knowledge management?
- How do data and information convert into knowledge and vice versa?
- What factors impact the conversion process of the three components?
- How can data, information and knowledge be effectively exploited in the use of ICT to support knowledge management?

The initiation, development, and implementation of effective KM projects is critical for modern organizations. There are, however, numerous issues around the process of successfully initiating, developing and implementing knowledge management projects (Brown and Duguid, 2000; KPMG, 2000; Rollo and Clarke, 2001; Davenport and Probst, 2002; Baalen et al., 2005; Teo, 2005). To better understand this process and the critical success factors for implementing knowledge management projects, this study defines another set of subsidiary research questions as follows:

- What factors have impacted on the implementation of ICT-based knowledge management projects?
- How can ICT be combined with non-technological elements in successfully implementing a knowledge management project?
- How can a ICT-based knowledge management project be effectively implemented?

These two sets of subsidiary questions together investigate the different aspects of the role of ICT in effective knowledge management. The first set of questions focuses on knowledge itself. The second set of questions focuses on knowledge management projects, and looks at linkages and interactions among different elements in organizational knowledge management.

1.3   Research objectives

The overall objective of this research is to better understand the role of ICT in knowledge management. The better understanding of the role of ICT in knowledge management will help facilitate the utilization of ICT in knowledge management, facilitate the maximization of the potential of ICT in knowledge management, and provide an effective guide for successfully implementing knowledge management projects. In seeking to find answers to the research questions defined above, this study employs a theoretical research framework based on a comprehensive literature review of knowledge, knowledge management and the use of ICT in knowledge management. This theoretical framework adopts a broad view of knowledge, which integrates knowledge objects and knowledge processes, while taking the knowledge environment into consideration. Two sets of hypotheses discussed in detail in Chapter 3 are put forward in regard to the research questions. This research, therefore, has a number of specific objectives, listed as follows:

- To test the theoretical research framework and hypotheses.
- To gain a better understanding of the relationships between ICT and knowledge management, and to develop a theoretical knowledge management framework to reflect the new understanding gained.
- To analyze the factors impacting on the conversion of knowledge objects and on the knowledge management processes.
- To identify the factors impacting on the role of ICT in knowledge management in order to realize the full potential of ICT in support of knowledge management.
- To identify the technologies and tools likely to facilitate the conversion of knowledge objects and knowledge management processes.

1.4   Research rationale

This research adopts a broad view of knowledge, extends existing knowledge conversion models, and proposes a theoretical research framework for facilitating a better understanding of the role of ICT in organizational knowledge management. The framework not only integrates knowledge objects and knowledge processes, but also takes the knowledge environment into consideration in the process of effective organizational knowledge management. As such, the framework provides a solid conceptual foundation for this research with a more comprehensive and balanced view on knowledge and knowledge management in organizations.

By exploring the use of ICT in knowledge management under the proposed framework, this research aims to gain a better understanding, theoretically, of the role of ICT in knowledge management and of the factors facilitating and hindering knowledge management. The research will have implications for the practical application of ICT in knowledge management in order to leverage the value of knowledge within organizations. The investigation of the role of ICT in knowledge management will provide support for organizations seeking to justify investments in ICT. The review of ICT used in the specific phases and processes of knowledge management will identify the applicability of the tools available, and suggest ways to integrate social systems and technical systems in a context of ongoing technological development.

Generally, this research examines the nature of knowledge and knowledge management, the relationship between knowledge, information and data, the conversion among these major constructs, and the role of ICT in knowledge management. More specifically, it focuses on the factors and aspects affecting the utilization of ICT in knowledge management, in conjunction with the conversion process involving data, information and knowledge.

1.5   Research methodology

This study adopts a hybrid research methodology in order to achieve the research objectives as stated above. This methodology, largely qualitative and interpretive, consists of theoretical induction, continuous literature review, secondary data analysis, and the conduct of an online questionnaire survey and a case study.

A research framework is established based on the literature review and theoretical induction. A questionnaire survey and a case study are conducted to obtain empirical data and to test and validate research hypotheses. To get a better understanding of current knowledge management best practices, secondary data are gathered and analyzed. In order to investigate the conversion of knowledge objects, an online survey is used to explore the experience, perceptions and opinions of respondents on the use of electronic resources at an individual level. To identify the factors that can determine success or failure in implementing knowledge management projects, a case study is undertaken to collect and analyze empirical evidence from the field.

In this methodology, the combination of quantitative and qualitative techniques allows the triangulation of the research findings and enhances the robustness and rigor of the research.

1.6   Significance of the research

The findings of this research will contribute to a better understanding of the role of ICT in knowledge management, and provide a useful guide to the effective use of ICT in enabling and supporting organizational knowledge management. It will also assist organizations in identifying those factors likely to be most critical to the success of knowledge management initiatives supported by ICT, and thus help to maximize their chances of success. Although having a direct focus on knowledge management and on ICT, this study takes account of internal environment factors in providing both guidelines for the implementation of knowledge management and mechanisms for its evaluation.

The knowledge management framework developed in this study can serve as a base from which an organization can launch knowledge management initiatives. Under the guidelines of this framework, knowledge management practitioners can choose the appropriate technology for their knowledge management strategy and identify the strengths and weaknesses in their organizational knowledge management practices. The framework could provide practitioners in the field of knowledge management with a roadmap for planning and implementing knowledge management projects. The interactive and holistic approach developed in this study will be of value both to practitioners seeking to plan for and implement knowledge management in their organizations, and to researchers interested both in knowledge management technologies and in the wider aspects of knowledge management.

1.7   Outline of the book

This book consists of ten chapters, shown as in Figure 1.2. Chapter 1 provides an overview of the research and of the organization of the book. It introduces the background to the research, presents the research questions, and explains the objectives and rationale of the research. This chapter also specifies the methodology employed and the significance of conducting this research. An outline of this book is presented at the end of the chapter.

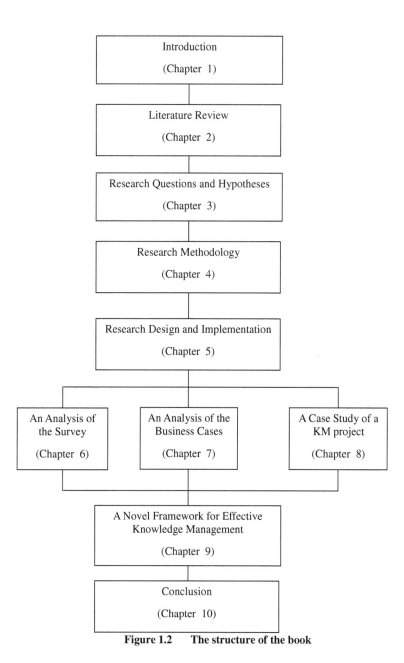

Figure 1.2   The structure of the book

Chapter 2 reviews the relevant literature pertaining to existing theories and practices of knowledge management. It introduces the focus and context of the research, and examines the nature of knowledge and knowledge management. This provides the basis for a conceptual foundation for this research. The chapter highlights the different approaches to knowledge management, with an emphasis on the application of technological approaches to knowledge management.

Chapter 3 presents the main research question and the sub-questions in detail. It describes a theoretical research framework for this study. Within the research framework, research hypotheses are proposed in relation to the research questions, and the objectives of the research are refined.

Chapter 4 examines a range of research approaches to, and strategies for, conducting research of various kinds. It assesses the suitability and appropriateness of these approaches and strategies for this particular study. On the basis of this discussion, this chapter proposes a hybrid approach for this study. The justification for developing such an approach is also presented.

Chapter 5 specifies the design and implementation for the quantitative and qualitative research employed in this study. It discusses design of the questionnaire, selection of the sample, survey procedures and protocols, the collection of data, and the analysis of data from the online survey. It also covers the design of interview questions, the selection of the case, the procedure and protocols for the case study, data collection from primary and secondary cases, and data analysis for case studies. The emphasis is on consistency in ensuring the validity and reliability of the research findings.

Chapter 6 presents the research findings based on an online survey for investigating the conversion of status between information and knowledge in a university environment. The data collected are analyzed to explore the characteristics of the conversion process, and to identify the factors influencing the process. The results of the survey show that the conversion of information into knowledge occurs during the use of electronic resources. It shows that different users with different purposes, play significantly different roles in the process of using electronic resources. More specifically, the relevance and the quality of information available are the most important factors affecting the use of electronic resources. The findings suggest that the use of ICT to convert information into knowledge will be highly valued when it takes account of the interest and purposes of the users, and serve different users by providing relevant and quality information.

Chapter 7 introduces an analysis of a variety of successful business cases in knowledge management to demonstrate best practices in knowledge management. It analyzes secondary data relevant to knowledge management projects. Business cases are drawn from a variety of industries and areas, with an emphasis on projects using ICT. Based on the theoretical research framework proposed in Chapter 3, pertinent issues that occur when undertaking knowledge management projects are analyzed and highlighted. Knowledge objects incorporated and knowledge management processes supported are discussed, and a range of critical success factors for knowledge management projects are summarized.

Chapter 8 summarizes 'lessons learned' from an unsuccessful implementation of a knowledge management project in a university environment. It uses a field case study of the pilot implementation of a knowledge portal in a university setting, to highlight and illustrate the critical success factors for implementing a knowledge management project. The case demonstrates that non-technological elements are often more critical for the successful implementation of knowledge management projects.

Chapter 9 summarizes the findings from the secondary data analysis, case study and online survey with respect to the role of ICT in knowledge management. It argues that there is no simple single approach by which organizations can attain effective use of ICT in knowledge management. A novel framework for successfully implementing knowledge management projects is proposed, based on the research. It outlines what the effective use of ICT in a knowledge management project requires.

Chapter 10 summarizes the findings of this study and presents the main contributions of this research to the development of knowledge management theory and practice. It also discusses the limitations of this research and point outs some directions for future research.

Chapter 2

Literature Review

2.1 Introduction

It is a widely recognized view that knowledge has become a primary source of firms' competitiveness (Drucker, 1988; Alavi, 1999; Bolisani and Scarso, 1999; Zack, 1999; Davenport and Prusak, 2000; Lehaney et al., 2004; Cepeda, 2006). Having and being able to effectively use organizational knowledge enables modern organizations to maintain and develop sustainable competitive advantages (Davenport and Prusak, 1998; Alavi, 1999; Zack, 1999).

The wide recognition that knowledge is the key to organizational success has led to the popularity of knowledge management in recent decades (Alavi, 1999; Bolisani and Scarso, 1999; Zack, 1999; Lehaney et al., 2004; Cepeda, 2006). Knowledge management is the process of systematically acquiring, organizing, disseminating and applying knowledge to achieve strategic aims of an organization. It is a means for organizations to leverage this valuable and strategic organizational source for achieving their organizational objectives. Knowledge management is widely used to support innovation, to capture insights and experiences, to reuse expertise, to foster collaboration, to improve the quality of decision making, and to increase the effectiveness of knowledge work (KPMG, 1999; Lehaney et al., 2004; Cepeda, 2006).

The rapid development of ICT offers unprecedented capacity for organizations to effectively make use of their knowledge. As a result, numerous applications of

ICT in knowledge management have been reported in the literature (Rollo and Clarke, 2001; Lehaney et al., 2004; Cepeda, 2006). For example, data mining suites use a combination of machine learning, statistical analysis, modeling techniques to detect hidden patterns and subtle relationships in data and infer rules that allow the prediction of future results (Dalkir, 2005).

The use of ICT in knowledge management, however, has had mixed results, with some projects successful and others unsuccessful (Davenport et al., 1998; Brown and Duguid, 2000; Rollo and Clarke, 2001; Davenport and Probst, 2002; Baalen et al., 2005; Teo, 2005; Tsui, 2005). This inevitably has cast doubt on the role of ICT in knowledge management. As a result, there is a need for further investigation of the role of ICT in knowledge management and of factors inhibiting and facilitating realization of the potential of ICT in knowledge management.

This chapter presents a review of the literature related to knowledge, knowledge management and the use of ICT in knowledge management to pave the way for this study. The chapter starts with a detailed discussion on the complex nature of knowledge. It then conducts an analysis of current knowledge management theory and practice, in particular relating to the use of ICT for supporting organizational knowledge management. To reinforce the case for this study, the chapter finally points out the issues and concerns regarding effective knowledge management using ICT.

2.2   The complexity of knowledge

Despite the recent decades of interest in knowledge management, knowledge is not a new concept (Nonaka and Takeuchi, 1995; Wiig, 1997; Kakabadse et al., 2003; Lehaney et al., 2004; Dalkir, 2005; Hislop, 2005; Cepeda, 2006; Prusak, 2006). For centuries, philosophers have been exploring the nature and the source of knowledge. Nonaka and Takeuchi (1995) trace the history of western philosophy and point out that there has long been a tradition separating the subject who 'knows' from the object that is 'known'. Descartes, who posited the "Cartesian split" between subject and object, formed the basis of this tradition. Following this tradition, knowledge can be viewed from two broad camps: an objective view and a subjective view (Becerra-Fernandez et al., 2004; Hislop, 2005). According to the objective view, reality is independent of human perceptions and can be structured in terms of *a priori* categories and concepts. According to the subjective view, on the other hand, reality is socially constructed through interactions with individuals (Schultze, 1999). Different perspectives can find their roots in the objective and subjective views (Becerra-Fernandez et al., 2004). Figure 2.1 shows the two broad views, and various perspectives on knowledge and their connections.

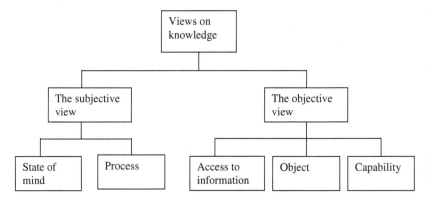

Figure 2.1   Two broad views on knowledge

Knowledge can be viewed as a condition of having access to information, as an object, or a capability. These perspectives belong to the objective view. Viewing knowledge as 'object' or 'entity' implies that knowledge can be captured, stored, manipulated, and transferred (Carlsson et al., 1996; McQueen, 1998; Zack 1998a; Alavi and Leidner, 2001). A condition of having access to information is just an extension of the view of knowledge as an object, with a special emphasis on the accessibility of the knowledge objects (Alavi and Leidner, 2001). Viewing knowledge as a capability places the emphasis on the application of knowledge to influence action.

Viewing knowledge as a process and viewing knowledge as a state of mind have a subjective view on knowledge. Viewing knowledge as a process emphasizes the process of knowing and the flow of knowledge that is continually emerging through practice. Considering knowledge as a state of mind focuses on the personal beliefs of individuals (Carlsson et al., 1996; Sveiby, 1997; Song et al., 2004). It is the primacy of human perception that makes these two perspectives as subjective. Table 2.1 summarizes the characteristics of knowledge from the objective and subjective views.

Table 2.1   The characteristics of knowledge

The Objective View	The Subjective View
Object/thing/commodity/entity	Process/flow/practice
Independent of human perceptions	Dependent of human perceptions
Impersonal	Personal/Social

Many typologies of knowledge in the literature of knowledge management, listed in Table 2.2, can be classified according to these two main categories: subjective knowledge and objective knowledge. For example, the well-known dichotomy between explicit and tacit knowledge can fall within the views of subjective and objective. Explicit knowledge is regarded as objective, independent of individuals and able to be codified into a tangible form. Tacit knowledge, on the other hand, is regarded as subjective, dependent on individuals and difficult to articulate (Nonaka and Takeuchi, 1995; Hislop, 2005). Table 2.3 categorizes the different types of knowledge according to the subjective and objective views.

Although the two main categories can accommodate the majority of types of knowledge, it is noted that some types of knowledge may fall into both categories or conversely may be difficult to place into either category. For example, the popular tacit-explicit dichotomy drawn from the work of Polanyi, ignores the fact that he identified a third category which he called implicit knowledge. Implicit knowledge is not explicit, but can be articulated. It is possible for people to share implicit knowledge (Firestone and McElroy, 2003).

Table 2.2   Taxonomies of knowledge

References	Categories of Knowledge
Anderson (1983), Zack (1998b)	Declarative, Procedural, Causal, Conditional, Relational
Blacker et al. (1993)	Embodied knowledge, Embrained knowledge, Encultured knowledge, Embedded knowledge, Encoded knowledge
Collins (1993)	Symbolic-type knowledge, Embodied knowledge, Embrained knowledge, Encultured knowledge
Musgrave (1993)	Knowledge of things and objects, Knowledge of how to do things, Knowledge of statements or propositions
Nonaka (1994)	Tacit knowledge, Explicit knowledge; Individual knowledge, Shared or collective knowledge
Lundvall (1996), Yim et al. (2004)	Know-what, Know-why, Know-how, Know-who
Millar et al. (1997)	Catalogue knowledge--know-what, Explanatory knowledge--know-why, Process knowledge--know-how, Social knowledge--know-who, Experiential knowledge--know-what was
Fleck (1997)	Formal knowledge, Instrumentalities, Informal knowledge, Contingent knowledge, Tacit knowledge, Meta-knowledge
Blumentritt and Johnson (1999)	Codified knowledge, Common knowledge, Social knowledge, Embodied knowledge

Table 2.3   Two main categories of knowledge

Objective Knowledge	Subjective Knowledge
Explicit knowledge	Tacit knowledge
Declarative knowledge	Procedural knowledge, causal knowledge, conditional knowledge, relational knowledge
Know-what	Know-how, know-why, know-who, know-what was
Catalogue knowledge	Process knowledge, explanatory knowledge, social knowledge, experiential knowledge
Encoded knowledge	Embodied knowledge, embrained knowledge, encultured knowledge, embedded knowledge
Formal knowledge	Informal knowledge, contingent knowledge

Researchers from different disciplines attempt to approach the field of knowledge management from different views and focus on certain aspects of knowledge and knowledge management. One common approach, particularly evident amongst information systems researchers, addresses the question of defining knowledge by distinguishing among knowledge, information, and data (Alavi and Leidner, 2001; Becerra-Fernandez et al., 2004; Hislop, 2005). Data can be defined as raw numbers, images, words, or sounds which are derived from observation or measurement. Information, in comparison, represents data arranged in a meaningful pattern, and data where some intellectual input has been added. Knowledge can be seen as data or information with a further layer of intellectual analysis added, where it is interpreted, meaning is attached, or where it is structured and linked with existing systems of beliefs and bodies of knowledge (Becerra-Fernandez et al., 2004; Hislop, 2005).

Data, information, and knowledge are interrelated dynamically and interactively. Different people may develop different interpretations of the same information and data. Information and data in a certain circumstance may be knowledge in another circumstance. Therefore, it is often difficult to distinguish these three terms (Davenport and Prusak, 1998; Tuomi, 2000; Alavi and Leidner, 2001; Song et al., 2003; Spiegler, 2003; Hislop, 2005). In a broad sense, they are all objects of knowledge management in that data and information can provide the building blocks of knowledge. However, a clear boundary can be drawn between information and knowledge where knowledge can only exist within the human mind (Blumentritt and Johnston, 1999).

An understanding of the concept of knowledge and of knowledge taxonomies is important for research and practice in knowledge management (Alavi and Leidner, 2001). The distinction among the different types of knowledge influences the theoretical developments in the knowledge management area. The various perspectives on knowledge suggest different approaches to managing the knowledge for knowledge management researches and practices.

Numerous definitions, perspectives and taxonomies of knowledge in the literature of knowledge management reveal various dimensions and characteristics of knowledge, and display the complexity and multi-faceted nature of knowledge (Nonaka and Takeuchi, 1995; Davenport and Prusak, 1998; Alavi and Leidner, 2001; Song et al. 2004). There is no broad categorical agreement, but there is a kind of consensus that accommodates the co-existence of different definitions of knowledge. This has implications for knowledge management researchers and practitioners both in terms of a general understanding of knowledge management and in making full use of that knowledge management potential that is so critical to organizations in today's dynamic environment.

2.3   Knowledge management theory and practice

Knowledge management includes management of knowledge and management of the processes for creating, organizing, transferring and sharing knowledge throughout the organization (Wiig, 1993; Davenport and Prusak, 2000; Lee and Kwok, 2000; Liebowitz, 2001; Dayasindhu, 2002; Nemati et al., 2002; Wickramasinghe and Mills, 2002; Wijetunge, 2002; Berdrow and Lane, 2003; Yang and Wan, 2004). Knowledge management aims at achieving the objectives of an organization through a systemic process of managing and utilizing knowledge within an organization.

Knowledge management as an organizational innovation has been around for more than a decade. It involves a wide range of disciplines and has attracted many researchers and practitioners. Philosophical perspectives embrace issues of what can be known and of truth. Ontological and epistemological positions can be broadly categorized as objective or subjective as discussed in the aforementioned section. In a sociological context, the study of knowledge is located within the broader category of culture, a construct that expresses the collective experiences of entire societies as well as of particular groups, classes, regions and communities. The influx of ideas from economics into knowledge management has not always followed a direct route, nor have the sources always been located within economics mainstream, but they have been significant. A major source of influence has been the literature on the resource-based theory of the firm (Martin, 2007).

In the resource-based view, organizations are regarded as heterogeneous bundles of imperfectly mobile resources and capabilities. Organizations seek to exploit knowledge by building these capabilities and related competencies. The emergence of the knowledge-based view has extended the resource-based view, arguing that the presence of knowledge itself and the process of utilization of knowledge to create knowledge in organizations may be the key inimitable resource to generate sustainable rent (Grant, 1996; Spender, 1996; Assudani, 2005).

Organizational learning is another significant and growing body of literature that has contributed to knowledge management. Organizational learning can be defined as the capacity or processes within an organization to maintain or improve performance based on experience (Nevis et al., 1995). This learning can occur by accident or design, in formal and less formal fashion and from doing (Nidumolu et al., 2005). Learning organizations can be viewed as organizations skilled at creating, acquiring and transferring knowledge, and at modifying their behaviour to reflect new knowledge and insights, or alternatively as organizations where knowledge is captured and systematized to the benefit of the entire organization (Garvin, 1993). As a concept, the learning organization still attracts a fair amount of criticism (Crossan et al, 1999). But no organization today can afford to abstain from the processes of individual and group learning and related efforts or ignore the need to embed the results in non-human repositories such as routines, systems, structures, culture and strategy (Garvin, 1993; Crossan et al., 1999).

A number of mechanisms for the learning process can be identified ranging from Argyris and Schon's original single and double loop learning (1978), through the exploitation of mental models within the organization (Kim, 1993) and the sharing of experiences and routines (Darr et al., 1995; Sorenson, 2003) including through the use of teams, communities and alliances (Mowery et al., 1996), and changes in organizational design (Audia et al., 2001; Sorenson, 2003), employing After-Action reviews and Lessons Learned (Botkin, 1999), and learning by hiring (Dosi, 1988; Kim, 1997; Song et al., 2003).

In line with the diversity of interdisciplinary perspectives on knowledge management, there is an abundance of frameworks, models, approaches, strategies, and technologies in the practice of knowledge management. Over the years a number of frameworks for the practice of knowledge management have emerged, many of them containing variations of familiar knowledge management processes (Wiig, 1997; Davenport and Prusak, 1998; Leonard-Barton, 1999; Tiwana, 2000). These frameworks are both generic and specific in scope, the former characterizing the various elements within frameworks, and the latter aimed at specific aspects of knowledge management such as knowledge conversion or transfer (Demarest, 1997; van der Spek and Spijkervet, 1997; Holsapple and Joshi, 1999). Those frameworks can also be descriptive in nature, identifying key knowledge management phenomena, or prescriptive in that they prescribe methodologies for the conduct of knowledge management (Beckman, 1997). They can also be compared on both a context and content dimension. The context dimension refers to the focus or primary intent of the framework, and the latter to knowledge resources and those activities and factors that facilitate its management. Typically contained within these frameworks are the most important knowledge management processes and sub-processes to do with the creation or acquisition of knowledge, its organization, storage, transfer and use. They have, however, been subject to criticism on the grounds that they have paid much less attention to knowledge resources, their interrelationships and manipulation (Holsapple and Joshi, 2002).

The frameworks that look beyond the enumeration of elements to consideration of the broader management implications cover those that specifically include core capabilities, such as employee knowledge and skills and organizational norms and values along with knowledge activities such as problem solving and knowledge importance (Leonard-Barton, 1995; Holsapple and Joshi, 1999). Others offer deeper insights by identifying a four-stage knowledge management cycle that runs from 'conceptualise', through, 'reflect', then 'act' to 'retrospect', addressing core issues of knowledge management in internal and external environments in a problem-solving context (van der Spek and Spijkervet, 1997; Holsapple and Joshi, 1999).

To be a valuable resource to an organization, knowledge must be created, captured, formalized, disseminated, shared and applied. Within the knowledge management cycle, there have been many models created to depict knowledge management processes (Bontis, 2001; Al-Ali, 2002; Skyrme, 2003). McAdam and McMreedy (1999) classified knowledge management models into three categories: knowledge category, intellectual and social construction. For example, Nonaka and Takeuchi's SECI model is a knowledge category model; Skandia Financial Services created its intellectual capital model; Firestone and McElroy (2003) proposed a socially constructed model, which links knowledge intrinsically with the social and learning processes within an organization. Although models provide insights and opportunities for analysis and reflection, they can be prescriptive and contextual and are based on the perceptions of individuals at certain points in time.

Knowledge management is largely regarded as a process involving various activities to deal with knowledge (Alavi and Leidner, 2001). These knowledge management activities range from knowledge generation, and codification to transfer of knowledge (Ruggles, 1997; Alavi and Leidner, 2001). Knowledge generation involves the acquisition, synthesis, and creation of knowledge. Knowledge codification includes capture, representation, transformation and storing of knowledge. Knowledge transfer comprises the retrieval, dissemination, sharing, access, visualization, reuse, application, clustering and summarization of knowledge.

Although different knowledge management processes are delineated in the literature, the underlying concepts are similar (Benbya et al., 2004). Table 2.4 shows some of the most common knowledge management processes appearing in the literature. Alavi and Leidner (2001) consider the four basic processes to be those of creating, storing and retrieving, transferring, and applying knowledge. These major processes can be further subdivided into creating internal knowledge, acquiring external knowledge, and storing knowledge in documents versus storing in routines (Teece, 1998), as well as updating the knowledge and sharing knowledge internally and externally.

Table 2.4   Knowledge management processes

References	Knowledge Management Processes
Wiig (1993)	Creation, manifestation, use, transfer
Nonaka and Takeuchi (1995)	Socialization, internalization, externalization, combination
Arthur Andersen and APQC (1996)	Share-create, identify, collect, adapt-organize, apply
Ruggles (1997)	Generation, codification, transfer
Van der Spek and Spijkervet (1997)	Develop, distribute, combine, hold
Angus et al. (1998)	Gathering, organizing, refining, disseminating
Gartner Group (1998)	Create, organize, capture, access, use
Holsapple and Joshi (1998)	Acquisition, selection, internalization, use
Jackson (1999)	Gathering, storage, communication, synthesis, dissemination
Davenport and Prusak (2000)	Generate, codify, transfer
Tyndale (2000)	Creation, organization, distribution, application
Wensley (2000)	Generation, codification, refinement, transmission
Alavi et al. (2001)	Creating, storing/retrieving, transferring, applying
Mertins et al. (2001)	Create, store, distribute, apply

Knowledge management activities are interrelated and integrated to generate and maintain the knowledge flow or cycle in organizations. Researchers and practitioners in knowledge management have developed many models to depict the relationships of these knowledge management activities. As illustrated in Figure 2.2, the SECI knowledge conversion spiral model (Nonaka and Takeuchi, 1995) is oft cited in the knowledge management literature. In this model, there are four modes of knowledge conversion: (a) from tacit knowledge to tacit knowledge, which is referred to as socialization; (b) from tacit knowledge to explicit knowledge, which is referred to as externalization; (c) from explicit knowledge to tacit knowledge, which is referred to as internalization, and (d) from explicit knowledge to explicit knowledge, which is referred to as combination. These processes are continuous and dynamic interaction between tacit and explicit knowledge occurs throughout the four quadrants, forming a knowledge spiral driving the knowledge flow. However, this model only focuses on the knowledge transformation between tacit and explicit knowledge and does not address other activities involved in managing knowledge.

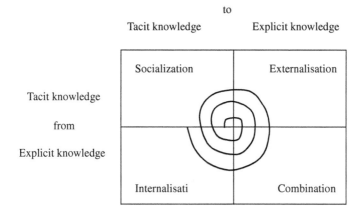

Figure 2.2   The SECI knowledge conversion spiral

The knowledge management literature has paid increasing attention to strategic issues. This includes work on knowledge management and knowledge-based strategies at enterprise, group and individual level (Bhatt, 2002; Maier and Remus, 2002; Russ et al., 2006), and on knowledge management as an element in or support for various business strategies. Under the influence of resource and knowledge-based theory, the emphasis in strategy has shifted from a product/market positioning perspective to one based on resources and capabilities that can be leveraged across a range of products and markets (Prahalad and Hamel, 1990; Zack, 1990; Barney, 1991; Grant, 1991; Collis and Montgomery, 1995; Allee, 2000; Carlisle, 2000; Zack, 2002). Strategic knowledge management is a process that links organizational knowledge with the design of organizational structures that foster knowledge, business strategy and the development of knowledge workers (Ordonez de Pablos, 2002). Current taxonomies of knowledge strategies include Earl's typology and categories in terms of opposites, such as exploitative and explorative strategies, codification and personalization strategies, survival and advancement strategies, external acquisition and internal development, and others such as product-process and brilliant design and master craftsman strategies (Levinthal and March, 1993; Bierly and Chakrabarti, 1996; Smith and Reinertsen, 1998; Hansen et al., 1999; Zack, 1999; Jones, 2000; Holden, 2001; Kluge et al., 2001; Lane et al., 2001; Parikh, 2001; Parise and Henderson, 2001; Schultz, 2001; Schultz and Jobe, 2001; Jones, 2002; Menor et al., 2002; Sakkab, 2002; Benner and Tushman, 2003; Cavalieri and Seivert, 2005).

When it comes to actual implementation of knowledge strategies, organizations tend to attempt a range of approaches to knowledge management. One convenient way of categorizing these strategies is to classify them into technological approaches and non-technological approaches. The technological approach to knowledge management employs ICT to support knowledge management in organizations. Such an approach aims to capture, codify, store, distribute and reuse explicit knowledge, abstract important tacit knowledge from context and make implicit knowledge explicit, portable, transferable, sharable and available through the use of ICT. Many knowledge management initiatives rely on ICT as an important enabler (Alavi and Leidner, 2001) for the effective use of organizational knowledge. For instance, the use of databases and data warehouses as the central repositories for capturing and storing information is common, and the use of email or group support systems is found to enable ubiquitous communication between members of an organization.

The non-technological approach to knowledge management emphasizes the managerial, organizational, social and cultural facets of knowledge management (O'Dell and Grayson, 1998; Malhotra, 1999; Davenport and Prusak, 2000). These approaches involve managing organizational changes, reviewing human resources policies, building informal networks or communities of practice, establishing knowledge-friendly environments and incentives to ensure knowledge workers get rewarded for fostering, creating and sharing their knowledge (Wickramasinghe, 2003). These knowledge management approaches recognize the subjective and social nature of knowledge and focus on the need for trust, and on norms and practices for sharing and applying tacit knowledge in order to create new knowledge through human interaction via social networks.

This classification reminds scholars of the fact that there are other alternatives to the widely adopted ICT-based approach to knowledge management. It also implies that different approaches can combine where a knowledge management perspective leads to the linking of knowledge and its management to key business processes. An appreciation of these wider issues can contribute to the success of ICT-based approaches.

2.4   ICT in knowledge management

A wide range of technologies and applications has featured within the ICT-based approach to knowledge management. Intranets, knowledge portals, content and document management systems, information retrieval engines, relational and object databases, electronic publishing systems, groupware and workflow systems, push technologies, help-desk applications, customer relationship management, data warehouse, data mining, business process reengineering, expertise networking, intelligent agents, conferencing, email, messaging, chat rooms, and knowledge creation applications have all been employed at one time or another (Marwick, 2001; Tyndale, 2002; Gray and Tehrani, 2003; Malafsky, 2003; Tsui, 2003). The leading vendors of knowledge management-related software and applications are in a market that was worth around $8.5 billion for knowledge management software and services in 2002 (Carnelley et al., 2001). Table 2.5 shows the available technologies contributing to knowledge management.

Table 2.5   Technologies contributing to knowledge management processes

Technologies	Functions	Contributing to Knowledge Management Processes
Content management	Store documents in a central library, control access to documents, keep an audit of activity and changes for the documents, search the content or index of the documents.	Collection, storage, distribution, dissemination
Data mining	Selecting, exploring, and modeling large amounts of data to identify and uncover previously hidden, untapped and unknown patterns	Creation, generation
Data warehouse	Central repository of information drawn from disparate and physically distributed operational source systems of an enterprise, as well as external data.	Extracting, cleansing, storing, capturing, coding, retrieving and sharing
Database management systems	Stores of information	Gathering, organizing, collecting, storage
Electronic publishing	Distribution of information in digital format	Dissemination
Groupware	Allowing people to communicate with each other, co-operate on projects and share information and knowledge.	Collaboration, communication, share
Information retrieval engines	Indexing, searching, and recalling recorded information.	Classification, index, search
Intelligent agents	Act on behalf of the human users to perform laborious information gathering tasks	Gathering, locating, access, filter, capture, synthesis, dissemination
Intranet	Organization-wide information distribution network	Capture, transfer, access, distribution
Portal	Gateway linking to many related sources	Access, share, collaboration
Push technologies	Sending relevant information to the users automatically	Distribution
Video conferencing	Allowing individuals and groups to share knowledge	Share, communication
Workflow systems	Automate business processes	Integration

These technologies employed in knowledge management can be categorized variously as knowledge management tools, information management tools, and knowledge management tools (Ruggles1997). A range of tools and technologies old and new is employed in knowledge management. This includes data and information as well as knowledge technologies (Ruggles, 1997; Tyndale, 2002). Table 2.6 shows categories of knowledge management tools based on Ruggles' classification (Ruggles, 1997).

Table 2.6   A classification of knowledge management tools

Categories	Functions	Tools
Knowledge generation	Acquisition from search engines to intelligent agents, Facilitating synthesis and development of relationships between concepts or ideas, Enabling creation	Grapevine, IdeaFisher, IdeaGenerator
Knowledge codification	Facilitating representation	Knowledge bases, Knowledge maps, organizational thesauri
Knowledge transfer	Clustering, summarization, natural language processing, visualization	Email, WWW, Messenger, video-conference, chat room, groupware, wireless technology, document/text management, intelligent agents, knowledge portal

Although it is necessary to distinguish knowledge management tools from data management tools and information management tools, these three categories of tools can be all employed in knowledge management. Marwick (2001) reviews technologies that contribute to knowledge management solutions based on Nonaka's tacit-explicit knowledge conversion model. Tyndale (2002) classifies knowledge management software tools into new tools and old tools. New tools have specifically been designed as knowledge management tools from their inception. Intranets, push technologies, agents, web portals, content management, groupware are some examples of the new tools. On the other hand, established data and information management tools have entered into the knowledge management arena with extended functionality. Databases, data mining, data warehousing, workflow systems are some examples of the old tools.

To emphasize those technologies that Ruggles classifies as knowledge management tools, Milton et al. (1999) point out that IT deals primarily with information, rather than with knowledge. Knowledge technology is needed to specifically orient towards knowledge. Compared to the technology that is a derivative of another tool or product and extends its functionality to support knowledge management, knowledge technology intends to be designed and developed to meet the needs in knowledge management from its inception.

Knowledge management systems (KMS) are information systems designed specifically to facilitate the sharing and integration of knowledge by focusing on creating, gathering, organizing, and disseminating an organization's "knowledge" as opposed to "information" or "data". They are not a single technology, but instead a collection of indexing, classifying and information-retrieval techniques coupled with methodologies designed to achieve results for the user. The key underpinning technologies enable: content and workflow management, which categorizes knowledge and directs it to workers who can benefit from it; search functionality, allowing users to look for relevant knowledge; and collaboration, to share knowledge (Purvis et al., 2001; Woods and Sheina, 1999). They are IT-based systems developed to support and enhance the organizational processes of knowledge creation, storage/retrieval, transfer, and application (Alavi and Leidner, 2001).

The objective of KMS is to support the creation, transfer, and application of knowledge in organizations (Alavi and Leidner, 1999), working in combination with existing information systems in organizations.

Despite reported successes of ICT-based knowledge management projects, many have failed (Malhotra, 2002; Tsui, 2005). One of the most heated debates in the knowledge management literature relates to the role that ICT can play in processes of knowledge management, which ranges from perspectives which suggest that ICT can play a crucial role, to diametrically opposed perspectives which argue that the nature of knowledge makes it impossible to share it electronically (Hislop, 2005).

The familiar 'productivity paradox' whereby organizations have not achieved the productivity gains expected from spending on IT may be equally valid in respect of knowledge management technologies (Douglas, 2002). Moreover, when it comes to the impact of knowledge management technologies on the improvement of organizational performance, critics are just as pessimistic (Lang, 2001). The existence of conflicting views on the impact of ICT on knowledge management performance merits the conduct of further investigation into the issues involved.

The dangers of over-emphasis on ICT are reinforced by additional concerns over the role of tacit knowledge. Johannessen et al. (2001) believe that the lack of empirical findings regarding the positive economic impact of ICT can be attributed to an undervaluing of the role of tacit knowledge. They argue for the need to focus on the total knowledge base including explicit knowledge and tacit knowledge in an organization. Ruggles (1998) reported that the greatest difficulty in knowledge management identified by the respondents to a survey was "changing people's behavior," and the biggest impediment to knowledge transfer was "culture." Ackerman (2000) states that there is a gap between technology and the social aspects of knowledge management, and refers to this situation as a "social technical gap." Marwick (2001) points out that effective knowledge management typically requires an appropriate combination of organizational, social, and managerial initiatives along with the deployment of appropriate technologies. To contribute effectively to knowledge management, technology must fit not only the purpose but also fit with the behaviour, work practices and cultures of the organizations involved.

2.5 Issues and concerns for effective knowledge management

Knowledge management research and practice have flourished in recent decades. In the theoretical field, numerous definitions, perspectives, and views on knowledge and knowledge management have been proposed, and progress in understanding the nature of knowledge has been made. Likewise, in practice, different strategies, approaches, methods, and tools have been adopted to achieve knowledge management objectives in organizations. However, there are still issues and concerns inhibiting the effective use of ICT in knowledge management.

Firstly, the complex nature of knowledge is extremely challenging for both researchers and practitioners, which contributes to the difficulty in applying ICT to knowledge management. Although philosophers have been discussing the issue since ancient times, the search for a formal definition of knowledge continues (Emery, 1997). Researchers from different disciplines attempt to approach the field of knowledge from different views (Kakabadse et al., 2003; Benbya, 2004; Prat, 2006). Many of these researches rest on the objective view and tend to privilege explicit over tacit knowledge, and knowledge possessed by individuals over that possessed by groups (Cook and Brown, 1999). These views often focus on certain aspects of knowledge and knowledge management. Despite the progress that has been made in understanding the nature of knowledge, there is no consensus yet on the definition of knowledge. The current understanding of the nature of knowledge and its implications for knowledge management is still far from satisfactory. The lack of clearly defined concepts acts as a hindrance for further research and practice in knowledge management. This contributes to the difficulty in applying ICT to knowledge management.

Secondly, the role of ICT in support of knowledge management and the impacting factors need to be further understood. There remains ample scope for further research into the role and impact of ICT in knowledge management. Although the technological approach is widely used in knowledge management and ICT has been recognized as an enabler, both the success and failure of knowledge management projects have been observed and documented. The understanding of the critical success factors for implementing ICT-based projects in knowledge management needs to be improved.

2.6 Concluding remarks

There is a wide variety of perception and interpretation of the nature of knowledge and knowledge management among researchers and practitioners. This proliferation of views has led to different frameworks, models, strategies, and approaches to knowledge management.

The technological approach characterized by extensive use of tools and systems, has still by no means succeeded either in silencing its critics or in demonstrating its effectiveness. In view of ongoing issues and concerns, the role of ICT in support of knowledge management still needs to be addressed and examined thoroughly.

Chapter 3

Research Questions and Hypotheses

3.1 Introduction

The complexity of knowledge and the drive to effectively make use of organizational knowledge have led to the development and adoption of different approaches to knowledge management (Blumentritt and Johnston, 1999; Hansen et al., 1999; Mentzas et al., 2001; Dalkir, 2005). The wide variety of approaches can conveniently categorized into two groups, namely, technological and non-technological approaches. The two categories of approaches are commonly present for effectively managing and making use of organizational knowledge (Meyer and Zack, 1996; Roos and Roos, 1997; Sveiby, 1997; Blumentritt and Johnston, 1999; Earl, 2001). The technological approach focuses on the employment of ICT for supporting and facilitating effective knowledge management activities including knowledge identification, codification, storing, and distribution and sharing (Ruggles, 1997; Song et al., 2005). The non-technological approach emphasizes socially based mechanisms such as communication and interaction between people, teams, communities, organizations and inter-organizations (O'Dell and Grayson, 1998; Malhotra, 1999; Davenport and Prusak, 2000; Vera and Crossan, 2003).

The adoption of the technological approach has led to the implementation of numerous knowledge management initiatives for effectively managing organizational knowledge (Kaplan and Norton, 1996; Civi, 2000; Walsham, 2001; Beccerra-Fernandez and Sabherwal, 2006). With the use of such an approach, knowledge management can be supported in sundry ways (Alavi and Leidner, 2001). For example, organizations can find an expert or a recorded source of knowledge from online directories and by searching databases. Virtual teams can work together and share knowledge. With the use of knowledge repositories, information on past projects can be easily accessed for team members undertaking similar projects. A picture of customer needs and behavior can be obtained by analyzing transaction data through data mining techniques (KPMG, 1998a). BULABS, an industrial pharmaceutical company in Memphis, Tennessee, uses an online interactive forum to respond to the changing basis of competition that has evolved from merely selling products to solving customers' chemical treatment problems (Zack, 1998a).

However, the use of ICT in knowledge management has mixed outcomes. Malhotra (2000) finds that there is no direct correlation between IT investments and knowledge management. The development and presence of the necessary technological infrastructure for organizational knowledge management does not guarantee the full utilization of the potential of ICT in knowledge management (Parlby, 1997; Malhotra, 2000; Walsham, 2001). This can lead to hesitation by practitioners as regards the full adoption and utilization of ICT-based initiatives due to the uncertain outcomes. The continued presence of such uncertainties means that there are strong grounds for further research into the relationships between ICT and knowledge management.

This chapter first proposes a theoretical framework for conducting the research. It states the objectives of this study, followed by a clear definition of the main research questions, sub-questions and the research hypotheses. The chapter finishes with some concluding remarks.

3.2   A theoretical research framework

Many knowledge management initiatives usually aim to leverage organizational knowledge and to support the process of managing knowledge (Hansen et al., 1999; Mentzas et al., 2001; Song et al, 2004). An object-centric view of knowledge and process-centric view of knowledge have often emerged in existing studies in knowledge management (Mentzas et al., 2001). For example, Nonaka and Takeuchi (1995) take an object-centric view of knowledge and have developed a well-known tacit-explicit knowledge conversion model for knowledge management. Ruggles (1998) and Alavi and Leidner (2001) adopt a process-centric view of knowledge in order to explore effective means for organizational knowledge management. Some researchers take a holistic view of knowledge and try to combine the object-centric view and the process-centric view (Mentzas et al., 2001; Maier and Remus, 2003). As a starting point to develop a research framework, this study takes a broad view of knowledge, which integrates object, process, resource and capacity into a holistic view (Song et al., 2004).

In this research, knowledge objects are viewed from an ICT perspective. They consist respectively of data, information and knowledge (Davenport and Prusak, 2000; Alavi and Leidner, 2001). Although knowledge can be categorized differently as discussed in Chapter 2, the three-element continuity used here has been preferred for its operational and practical relevance (Ein-Dor, 2006). Data are the objects represented, stored, processed and transferred in the computer and over the network. Information is the meaningful representation and interpretation of data in a generalized or standardized form. Knowledge is specific, actionable and valuable information in a special or customized form (Spiegler, 2003). Here they are all grouped as knowledge objects because (a) the three elements can be converted into each other; and (b) they are all objects of knowledge management (Song et al., 2003).

The relationship among data, information and knowledge is the cornerstone for understanding the role of ICT in knowledge management (Alavi and Leidner, 2001). However, it can at times be difficult to distinguish one from the other (Davenport and Prusak, 2000; Tuomi, 2000; Alavi and Leidner, 2001; Song et al., 2003; Spiegler, 2003), although in any case it is more important to understand the conversion between objects than to identify the distinctions amongst them. The nature of the conversion process needs to be understood in order to appreciate key processes in knowledge – capture and creation, storage, sharing, re-use and leveraging. Such understandings could contribute to the development of more effective applications of ICT in organizational knowledge management.

Although some subtle varieties of models present knowledge can be presented in wisdom... there are, there are two dominant models in the literature that are used to represent these relationships between knowledge objects. These are the conventional hierarchical model and the reversed hierarchical model (Davenport and Prusak, 2000; Tuomi, 2000; Song et al., 2003; Spiegler, 2003). Figure 3.1 shows these two models in details.

In the conventional hierarchical model, data are seen essentially as facts. These facts can be structured purposely to become information in a specific context (Hoffer et al, 2003). Information, in turn, becomes knowledge when it is interpreted or put into context, or when meaning is added to it (Davenport and Prusak, 2000; Alavi and Leidner, 2001; Song et al., 2003; Spiegler, 2003).

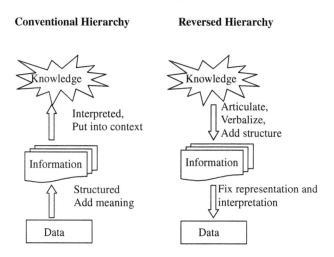

Figure 3.1   The knowledge conversion models

The reversed hierarchical model recognizes that data only emerge after information is available. Information only emerges after the required knowledge is present (Tuomi, 2000; Spiegler, 2003; Song et al, 2004). Knowledge must exist before information can be formulated and before data can be measured to form information. Knowledge exists which, when articulated, verbalized, and structured, becomes information which, when assigned a fixed representation and standard interpretation, becomes data (Tuomi, 2000).

To facilitate a better understanding of these two models, this research conducts a comparative study of the two models with respect to (a) the main streams of epistemology reflected, (b) the technology strategies that will be adopted, and (c) the knowledge conversions that will be supported.

Epistemology is the theory of knowledge. Positivism and constructivism are two main schools of epistemology. Positivism believes that knowledge can be obtained deductively by reasoning (Alavi and Leidner, 1999). The 'knowledge-information-data' hierarchy reflects this school of thought. It states that existing knowledge is based on absolute truth, on the basis of which information and data are formalized by employing reasoning mechanisms.

Constructivism believes that knowledge can be obtained inductively from sensory experiences (Nonaka and Takeuchi, 1995), emphasizing the extent to which knowledge is embedded within and inseparable from practice (Hislop, 2005). The 'data-information-knowledge' hierarchy reflects the constructivist epistemology. This line of thought is more common in the non-technological approach to knowledge management.

Both hierarchies can be used as a conceptual guide for the design and development of knowledge management systems for organizational knowledge management. With the 'data-information-knowledge' hierarchy, data mining techniques can be used to discover the pattern in the organizational data warehouse and to extract valuable knowledge emerging from these patterns (Shaw et al., 2001; Heinrichs and Lim, 2003). In the 'knowledge-information-data' hierarchy, knowledge transfer is a good example of data conversion (Drucker, 1993; Jarrar, 2002; Hall, 2003). This is because the transfer of knowledge can act as a guide to best practices for every organization to share. This facilitates knowledge sharing and organizational learning, which are arguably the critical elements of effective knowledge management (Pan and Leidner, 2003).

Two technology strategies, that is, the 'push' strategy and the 'pull' strategy, are often adopted in designing and developing organizational knowledge management systems (Nonaka, 1994; Grant, 1996; Spender, 1996). By using the 'pull' strategy, users are motivated to actively initiate the request for information and knowledge. With the use of the 'push' strategy, available information and knowledge are automatically delivered to the users without their intervention. Combining both strategies, individuals using the web are able to select the information they want while the information is 'broadcast' to them 'just-in-case' by a prescribed list (Burn et al., 2000).

The 'pull' technology strategy in knowledge conversion will generally be adopted based on the 'data-information-knowledge' model. Users request information and knowledge with respect to specific tasks or functions. Those users are not guaranteed to be satisfied either because this information and knowledge is not available or because results are not what users exactly expect. As the amount of data gathered in an organization is increasingly immeasurable, information overload is a real problem (Lewis, 1998; Burn et al., 2000; Turban et al., 2000). This constantly frustrates efforts at information reuse and knowledge sharing in an organization. For example, Turban et al. (2000) stated that information-overload reduces the decision-making capabilities of knowledge workers by 50%. Burn et al. (2000) show that the information overload associated with the installation of an enterprise resource planning (ERP) application had adversely affected the capacity of knowledge workers at SAP.

To address the information overload problem, the 'push' strategy is introduced in the 'knowledge-information-data' model (Gray and Tehrani, 2003). With the 'knowledge-information-data' model, users' preferences, specific tasks and functions can be identified, captured and guided by the existing knowledge. Requested information and data relevant to specific tasks and functions can be delivered to targeted users proactively, to give users exactly what they need. This ability to push data to users rather than making users find and pull data themselves enables the intended users to get what they want much more effectively. It also helps the users to configure the information to be captured, stored, and gathered.

Under the influence originally of Polanyi (1983) and then Nonaka and

Tackeuchi (1995) the classification of knowledge into tacit and explicit knowledge has become well recognized (Polanyi, 1983; Nonaka, 1994; Sveiby, 1997; Martin, 2004). While providing a useful vehicle for research and in some senses helpful in practice, this artificial dichotomy must be treated with caution. A tendency to see the concepts as absolute, along with the acceptance of an oversimplified and linear conversion process has resulted in many failed attempts at knowledge management through the inability to transfer tacit knowledge into explicit form. However, the knowledge socialization, externalization, combination, and internalization (SECI) model (Nonaka and Takeuchi, 1995) continues to be influential, although perhaps more in an explanatory than in a practical sense. Knowledge management theorists (Snowden, 2000; Snowden, 2002; Firestone and McElroy, 2003; Wiig, 2005) while acknowledging SECI's contribution would regard it as falling within first generation developments in knowledge management and, therefore as limited in relevance.

Within the operation of the SECI model and in a broad sense, data and information are subsets of explicit knowledge (Nonaka, 1996). The conventional hierarchy from 'data to information then to knowledge' reflects the process of internalization and combination (Nonaka and Takeuchi, 1995). The reversed hierarchy of 'knowledge to information to data' reflects the process of externalization and combination. However, these differing depictions of the relationships between data, information and knowledge represent only part of the picture of knowledge flow in an organization.

Several important issues in these two relationship models remain to be explored for a better understanding of these relationships in order to achieve effective knowledge management in an organization. For example, the lack of any direct relationship between data and knowledge is present in both models (Tuomi, 2000; Song et al., 2003; Spiegler, 2003). This can be seen as causing a discontinuity in knowledge transformation flows. Nevertheless, in knowledge management research and practice there is ample evidence for the existence of such a relationship in applications such as data mining, data warehouse and KMS (Frawley et al., 1992; Fayyad et al., 1996).

A broader issue is the continued incomplete understanding of the actual conversion processes between data, information and knowledge in either model (Firestone and McElroy, 2003; Song et al, 2003). The conversion processes involve the conversion from one source to another, from one state to another, from one form to another. For example, in the component of knowledge, knowledge may be transferred across different levels ranging from individual, group, team, functional department to organization, or across different repositories such as organization memory, knowledge base, human mind, and documents.

Another issue of concern is the hierarchical structure of these two models in the description of the relationships between data, information and knowledge (Song et al, 2003). This hierarchical structure may imply that one component is superior to another component. This can easily result in an over-emphasis on the perceived superior component and an overlooking of the others without awareness of the interrelationship and interaction effect of these constructs in knowledge management (Nonaka, 1996). Also the hierarchical structure of these two models seems to ignore the facility for reuse of available data, information and knowledge in an organization. This may result in insufficient attention being paid to the iteration of data or knowledge in the process of managing organizational knowledge through effective knowledge sharing (Butler, 2003).

The two existing models discussed above are opposing yet complementary to each other in terms of the different epistemological streams reflected, technological strategies adopted, and knowledge conversion processes supported. To address the issues discussed above for investigation of the role of ICT in the conversions among data, information and knowledge, this study proposes a more complete knowledge object conversion model, as shown in Figure 3.2.

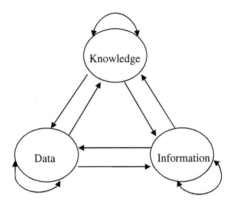

Figure 3.2   The knowledge object conversion model

The proposed model synthesizes the conventional hierarchy and the reversed hierarchy in order to facilitate a better understanding of the relationships between data, information and knowledge. It develops a holistic, dynamic and evolving cycle among the three constructs of data, information and knowledge in order to better depict the interrelationships among these knowledge objects. This proposed model becomes the theoretical framework for carrying out this research.

The conversion within each object may occur from one source to another such as from people to system, and from one form or state to another by means of updating, aggregating, sorting, indexing, clustering, classifying, codifying, storing, retrieving, transferring, and communicating. For example, the data format can be changed and existed in systems or documents. Different reports can be produced through sorting in the database. Knowledge can be shared by the members in a community of practice (Offsey, 1997; Bhatt, 2001; Hupic et al., 2002; Song et al., 2003).

In addition, every object in the model can be the starting point and also the end point of the knowledge conversion process (Song et al., 2003). Correspondingly, the model encompasses knowledge management, information management, and data management while accommodating the interaction effects of other objects.

Conversions between different objects will reflect the different activities and objectives, technologies and tools applied in an organization (Davenport, 1999; Butler, 2003; Song et al., 2003).

To better understand the processes of conversion among objects, this study focuses on the conversion process between information and knowledge since it is more problematic than others (Dretske, 1981; Alavi and Leidner, 2001). The other conversion processes are relatively less problematic in knowledge management practice. Examples of the conversion between data and knowledge can be seen in artificial intelligence, pattern abstraction, knowledge discovery, data mining, KMS, and knowledge repositories (Hasan and Crawford, 2003). The conversion between data and information is more commonly identified where information management applications, such as database management systems, management information systems, and data warehouse are employed (Davenport, 1999; Butler, 2003; Song et al., 2003).

Information turns into knowledge when it is interpreted and put into context by recipients (Tuomi, 2000; Spiegler, 2003). The context means everything relevant to the content. It helps a user interpret the implication for any specific purpose. It is generally accepted that knowledge can add value to information in an action or decision making context. In this regard, knowledge can be distinguished from information based on three dimensions: user, purpose and value (Song et al., 2006). Although there is no precise delineation point between information and knowledge, they provide a rudimentary form of metric for the transformation between information and knowledge.

When the content is right both for the purpose and the user, the value is regarded as high, and consequently, regarded as knowledge for the user and purpose in question. On the contrary, when the content is not right for either user or purpose, its value is not regarded as high and consequently, regarded as information for the user and purpose in question. Figure 3.3 shows these three dimensions.

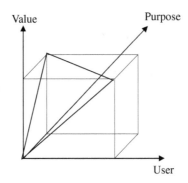

Figure 3.3   The information-knowledge conversion process

Any organization that desires to excel in managing knowledge has to perform well in knowledge processes. Ruggles (1997) groups activities taking place in the process into knowledge generation, knowledge codification and knowledge transfer. Angus et al. (1998) classify knowledge activities as knowledge gathering, organizing, refining and disseminating. Jackson (1999) divides activities into gathering, storage, communication, synthesis, and dissemination. While Wensley (2000) categorizes activities as generation, codification, refinement and transmission, Tyndale (2000) puts them into a knowledge development life cycle consisting of creation, organization, distribution, and application. The knowledge processes are composed of knowledge creation and knowledge integration (Firestone and McElroy, 2003). Despite slight discrepancies in the delineation of the processes appearing in the literature, Alavi and Leidner (2001) believe that creating, storing/retrieving, transferring, and applying knowledge are the four basic processes in organizational knowledge management.

To facilitate the implementation of this research, this study classifies knowledge management activities as knowledge generation, codification, transfer, and application. Table 3.1 shows the classification of knowledge management processes. Knowledge generation includes creation, acquisition, searching, capture, gathering, fusion, absorption, assimilation and adaptation. Codification involves categorization, cataloguing, filtering, linking, indexing, analysis, interpretation, amalgamation, and classification. Transfer consists of collaboration, dissemination, sharing, notifying, publishing, distribution, and transmission. Application is the process involving change, revision, amendment, and review.

Table 3.1   A classification of knowledge management processes

Processes	References
Generation	Generation (Ruggles, 1997 ; Wensley, 2000;), Gathering (Angus et al., 1998; Jackson,1999), Creation (Tyndale, 2000), Creating (Alavi et al., 2001)
Codification	Codification (Ruggles, 1997; Wensley, 2000), Organizing (Angus et al., 1998), Organization (Tyndale, 2000), Storage (Jackson,1999), Storing/Retrieving (Alavi et al., 2001), Refining (Angus et al., 1998), Refinement (Wensley, 2000)
Transfer	Transfer (Ruggles, 1997), Transferring (Alavi et al., 2001), Transmission (Wensley, 2000), Disseminating (Angus et al., 1998; Jackson,1999), Communication (Jackson,1999), Distribution(Tyndale, 2000)
Application	Application (Tyndale, 2000), Applying (Alavi et al., 2001), Synthesis (Jackson,1999)

This study examines the roles of ICT within each of these four knowledge management activities. Figure 3.4 illustrates the organizational knowledge management processes in a dynamic life cycle.

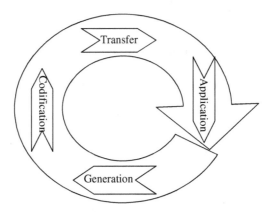

Figure 3.4   The knowledge management processes

Knowledge management processes manipulate knowledge objects in organizations in order to build knowledge capabilities to achieve organizational knowledge management objectives (Sveiby, 1997). Knowledge management processes are closely intertwined with knowledge objects, forming a dynamic life cycle of knowledge. This knowledge life cycle becomes the focus of organizational knowledge management and constitutes the core of knowledge management efforts (Davenport and Prusak, 2000; Alavi and Leidner, 2001).

The environment in which the knowledge life cycle occurs and evolves is critical for effective knowledge management efforts (Maier, 2004; Maier and Hadrich, 2006; Jennex, 2006). The cycle interacts with organizational environmental elements such as organizational strategy, resources, management, structure, culture, people and technology infrastructure while knowledge resources are deployed and knowledge capacity is built. For example, Hewlett-Packard (HP) alerts customers to the most frequently asked questions and provides solutions through a Lotus Notes database. By doing so, a HP project in the customer support area has reduced the cost of answering customers' calls by 50 percent in two years. This allows the company to hire less technically experienced support analysts (Davenport et al., 1998), resulting in the improvement of organization performance and leading to more satisfied customers. This study examines the role of ICT based on an integrated knowledge management model. Figure 3.5 shows the integrated knowledge management model in which knowledge objects and processes interact in a holistic way.

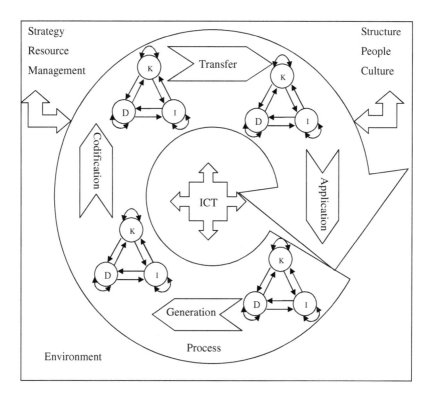

Figure 3.5   An integrated knowledge management model

3.3   Research objectives

By exploring and investigating the role of ICT in knowledge management and its critical success factors, this research aims to improve the performance of ICT investments, maximize potential of ICT in support of knowledge management, and guide the progress of knowledge management projects. In seeking to find answers to the research questions and to test research hypotheses, this research has a number of objectives. These objectives are:

- To test the theoretical research framework and hypotheses proposed.
- To gain a better understanding of the relationships between ICT and effective knowledge management.
- To analyze the factors impacting on the conversion of knowledge objects and on knowledge management processes.
- To identify critical success factors for the role of ICT in knowledge management.
- To identify the technologies and tools likely to facilitate the conversion of knowledge objects and knowledge management processes.

3.4   Research questions

Despite decades of research and practice there remain serious impediments to the effective use of ICT in knowledge management (Davenport, 1997; Alavi and Leider, 1999; Binney, 2001; Hupic et al, 2002). A review of the knowledge management literature reveals some confusion over the relationship between ICT and knowledge management, something which arguably has impacted adversely not only on understanding but also take-up of knowledge management. This research seeks to add clarification to and understanding of the role of ICT in knowledge management. The primary research question is:

What role can ICT play in knowledge management and how can ICT be effectively used in knowledge management?

Two sub-sets of subsidiary questions are developed from the perspectives of (a) knowledge objects and processes, and (b) knowledge management projects.

This research begins with an examination of the relationships between data, information and knowledge. Knowledge, information and data are constructs central to the technological dimension of knowledge management. Relationships among data, information and knowledge are commonly the starting point for investigating the use of ICT in knowledge management (Nonaka and Takeuchi, 1995; Davenport and Prusak, 2000; Alavi and Leidner, 2001; Song et al. 2004). A better understanding of the nature of knowledge and its relationship with data and information can help inform further research into the relationship between ICT, knowledge and knowledge management. Accordingly a first set of subsidiary research questions is developed as follows:

- What roles do data and information play in the use of ICT to support knowledge management?
- How do data and information convert into knowledge and vice versa?
- What factors impact the conversion process of the three components?
- How can data, information and knowledge be effectively exploited in the use of ICT to support knowledge management?

The initiation, development, and implementation of effective knowledge management projects are critical for modern organizations. There are, however, numerous issues around the processes of successfully initiating, developing and implementing knowledge management projects (Brown and Duguid, 2000; KPMG, 2000; Rollo and Clarke, 2001; Davenport and Probst, 2002; Baalen et al., 2005; Teo, 2005). To better understand these processes and the critical success factors for implementing knowledge management projects, this study defines another set of subsidiary research questions as follows:

- What factors have impacted on the implementation of ICT-based knowledge management projects?
- How can ICT be combined with non-technological elements in successfully implementing a knowledge management project?
- How can a ICT-based knowledge management project be effectively implemented?

These two sets of subsidiary questions together investigate different aspects of the role of ICT in effective knowledge management. The first set of questions focuses on knowledge and the processes of knowledge management. The second set of questions looks at linkages and interactions among different elements in organizational knowledge management. Figure 3.6 illustrates the focus and relationship of these research questions.

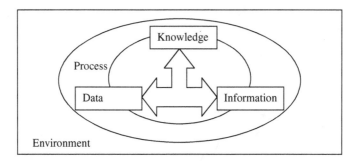

Figure 3.6   The focus of two sets of research questions

3.5   Research hypotheses

The role of ICT in support of knowledge management is examined not only in terms of the conversion of knowledge objects, but also in relation to knowledge processes. In addition, the environmental elements must be considered including cultural and organizational elements. Based on the integrated knowledge management model, two sets of research hypotheses are proposed:

H1   ICT can enable and facilitate the conversion of knowledge objects.

H1.1   ICT can enable and facilitate conversion processes between data and information.

H1.2   ICT can enable and facilitate conversion processes between data and knowledge.

H1.3   ICT can enable and facilitate conversion processes between information and knowledge.

H2   ICT must incorporate non-technological elements for the effective implementation of knowledge management projects.

H2.1   ICT must incorporate an organizational element for the

effective implementation of knowledge management
projects.

H2.2   ICT must incorporate a cultural element for the effective
implementation of knowledge management projects.

The link between primary research question, subsidiary questions, the integrated knowledge management model and hypotheses is shown in Figure 3.6.

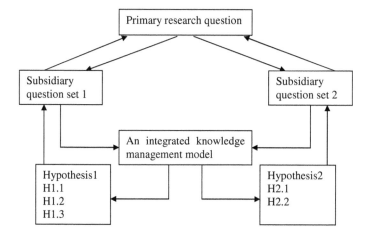

**Figure 3.7   The link of primary research question, subsidiary research
questions, the integrated knowledge management model, and hypotheses**

3.6   Concluding remarks

The literature review suggests that two main streams can be identified in knowledge management practice and research (Mentzas et al., 2001). They focus either on knowledge objects or on knowledge management processes. By combining these two main focuses, this chapter proposes an integrated knowledge management model as the theoretical research framework for this study.

Within this research framework, the role of ICT in knowledge management is examined not only in support of the conversion of knowledge objects, but also in support of knowledge processes. More importantly, the research seeks to explore the interaction between knowledge objects and knowledge processes for knowledge management.

Chapter 4

Research Methodology

4.1 Introduction

Knowledge, as a source of gaining and sustaining competitive advantage (Nonaka, 1994; Grant, 1996; Spender, 1996), has become increasingly important for organizations. The growing recognition that knowledge can add value to organizations drives numerous initiatives for effectively making use of organizational knowledge (Alavi, 1999; Bolisani and Scarso, 1999; Zack, 1999; Lehaney et al., 2004; Cepeda, 2006).

The rapid advance of ICT facilitates the effective use of organizational knowledge in a more organized manner (Lehaney et al., 2004; Cepeda, 2006). There are, however, conflicting results from the application of ICT in knowledge management reported in the knowledge management practices. Such conflicting results often lead to a misunderstanding of the role of ICT in knowledge management among researchers and practitioners. To ensure that ICT can be effectively utilized in knowledge management, it is important to understand the role of ICT in support of knowledge management. Such understanding can help explore answers to questions such as the role that ICT can play in support of knowledge management and how ICT can be effectively used in knowledge management.

In order to answer the research questions stated in Chapter 3 and to test the corresponding hypotheses, this study seeks an appropriate research methodology. This involves clarifying the approach and strategy for collecting and analysing data related to the research questions, considering the validity and reliability of the data collected, and evaluating the suitability of the analysis techniques chosen.

The selection of a research methodology for carrying out a specific research project is crucial to the success of the research project (Creswell, 1994; Corbetta 2003). Such a methodology can guide the conduct of the research and affect the quality of the research result. However, selecting an appropriate methodology for the research is not a simple task due to the availability of numerous methods, techniques, and procedures and the specific nature of the research project (Cooper and Emory, 1995; Saunders et al., 2000).

This chapter presents the methodology for carrying out the proposed research based on a research process that has been likened to the structure of an 'onion'. It explains the research philosophy adopted, the research approach flowing from the philosophy, the research strategy, and the time horizons applied to the research. It assesses the appropriateness of a range of methods that are likely to be available to help in answering the research questions and meeting the research objectives. After discussing the advantages and disadvantages of using these methods, and the ways of evaluating their validity and reliability, this chapter justifies the selection of the research method chosen.

4.2   Rationale for selecting the research methodology

Before deciding which methodology is suitable for this research, it is important to clarify some related issues underlying the choice of research methodology (Creswell, 1994; Corbetta 2003). These issues involve the research philosophy adopted, research approach flowing from the philosophy, research strategy and the time horizons applied to the research (Saunders et al., 2000). Figure 4.1 shows these issues as been stated in the previous paragraph.

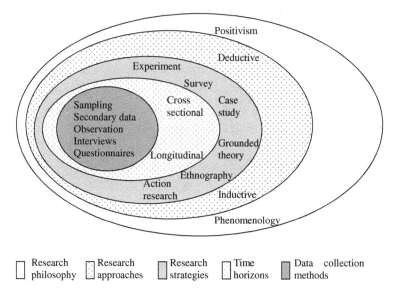

Figure 4.1   The research process

Natural scientists usually adopt the philosophical stance of 'positivism' (Creswell, 1994; Corbetta 2003). They act as objective and independent analysts without affecting or being affected by the subject of the research (Remenyi et al., 1998). Researchers in business and management, on the other hand, tend to adopt the philosophical stance of 'phenomenology' (Creswell, 1994; Corbetta 2003). They argue that the social world is far too complex to be explained in simple positivist terms. To understand such a complex world requires the discovery of all the details of the situation or the mechanisms behind such situations (Remenyi et al., 1998; Saunders et al., 2000).

During the course of its development, knowledge management has demonstrated a trans-disciplinary nature (Wiig, 1997; Kakabadse et al., 2003; Prat, 2006). There are a variety of disciplines that have influenced and offered many insights into the field of knowledge management. These disciplines range from economics, management science, organizational theory, strategic management, human-resources management, information science, knowledge engineering, artificial intelligence, philosophy, psychology, and educational science, to cognitive science (Kakabadse et al., 2003; Prat, 2006). While research into knowledge management often occurs in the region of natural science, it falls largely within the province of social, business and management science (Corbetta, 2003; Prusak, 2006). This suggests that this study should adopt a mixture of positivism and phenomenology, which is not unusual in business and management research (Creswell, 1994; Saunders et al., 2000; Corbetta 2003).

Two approaches commonly used in research are the deductive approach and the inductive approach (Creswell, 1994; Saunders et al., 2000; Corbetta 2003). With the use of the deductive approach, a theory is developed and hypotheses are proposed. The objective of the research using this approach is to design a research strategy in order to test the hypotheses (Creswell, 1994). The application of the inductive approach is to approach the research problem from the other end (Corbetta 2003). The use of the inductive approach emphasizes the development of a conclusion from one or more particular facts or pieces of evidence. The reasoning process is moving from the particular to the general. In the inductive approach, theory is derived from the data collected and from empirical observation (Saunders et al., 2000). Table 4.1 shows the major differences between these two types of approaches.

Table 4.1   A comparison between the deductive and the inductive approaches

Deductive emphasizes	Inductive emphasizes
• Scientific principles • Moving from theory to data • The need to explain causal relationships between variables • The collection of quantitative data • The application of controls to ensure validity of data • The operationalization of concepts to ensure clarity of definition • A highly structured approach • Researcher independence of what is being researched • The necessity to select samples of sufficient size in order to generalize conclusions	• Gaining an understanding of the meanings humans attach to events • A close understanding of the research context • The collection of qualitative data • A more flexible structure to permit changes of research emphasis as the research progresses • A realization that the researcher is part of the research process • Less concern with the need to generalize

This study aims primarily to test the research framework and hypotheses presented in Chapter 3. As a result, the deductive approach is appropriate. The proposed research, however, also involves analyzing the factors facilitating conversion between knowledge objects and knowledge management processes in organizational knowledge management. Such an investigation necessitates an understanding of the context and environment in which ICT is used to support organizational knowledge management. As such, the inductive approach is also an appropriate methodology for this research. As a consequence, both the deductive approach and the inductive approach are required in order to effectively achieve the objective of this research.

A research strategy defines the sources from which data are collected (Corbetta 2003). It provides a general plan to conduct a research project. Research methods, on the other hand, specify the details of data collection and analysis. In general, the research methods can be categorized as quantitative and qualitative research methods (Bryman and Bell, 2003).

Quantitative research methods emphasize quantification in the collection and analysis of data (Bryman and Bell, 2003). Such methods usually involve the use of statistical analysis in order to draw meaningful conclusions from the research (Ticehurst and Veal, 2000). Examples of quantitative methods are survey, experiment, and simulation. The data can be derived from using questionnaire surveys, from onsite observation or from analysing secondary data sources available in the public domain (Ticehurst and Veal, 2000).

The qualitative research method emphasizes the description of a scenario using words rather than the quantification of a phenomenon in the collection and analysis of data (Bryman and Bell, 2003). Examples of qualitative methods include case study, grounded theory, ethnography, and action research (Cooper and Emory, 1995; Saunders et al, 2000; Ticehurst and Veal, 2000; Bryman and Bell, 2003; Corbetta, 2003). The methods used to gather qualitative information include observation, informal and in-depth interviewing and participant observation (Ticehurst and Veal, 2000). Table 4.2 shows the fundamental differences between quantitative and qualitative research methods (Bryman and Bell, 2003).

Table 4.2   Differences between quantitative and qualitative research methods

Orientation	Quantitative	Qualitative
Principal orientation to the role of theory in relation to research	Deductive; Testing of theory	Inductive; Generation of theory
Epistemological orientation	Natural science model, in particular positivism	Interpretivism
Ontological orientation	Objectivism	Constructionism

Many researchers, however, believe that these two research methods complement one another in carrying out research projects of various kinds (Ticehurst and Veal, 2000). Saunders et al. (2000) advocate employing multiple methods in the same study and list two major advantages for doing so. The first is that different methods can be used for different purposes in a study, since each method has its unique strengths and weaknesses (Smith, 1975). The second is that the multi-method approach enables triangulation to take place. Utilising both quantitative and qualitative methods allows a researcher to gain a broader or more complete understanding of the issues being investigated. At the same time, the weaknesses of one method are complemented by the strengths of another (Saunders et al., 2000).

Cross-sectional studies allow research projects to be undertaken at a particular time, while longitudinal studies conduct research projects to observe any change over a period of time. Combining cross-sectional and longitudinal studies in a research project enables a snapshot taken at a particular time as well as a representation of events over a given period (Cooper and Emory, 1995; Saunders et al., 2000). For this particular study, the change and development of knowledge management project implementation can be tracked in the longitudinal study, while the cross-sectional study can present a broad picture of the use of ICT in support of knowledge management.

After all the outer layers of the research process 'onion' have been peeled away, the combination of quantitative and qualitative research techniques emerges as an advantageous option for this study. However, there is a wide range of these techniques available in the literature for carrying out this research. To help decide which combination is suitable, this study carefully considers the research purpose. Such a consideration is based on the identification of whether the purpose of this research is exploratory, descriptive, or explanatory (Saunders et al, 2000).

Exploratory studies are a valuable means to find out 'what is happening; to seek new insights; to ask questions and to assess phenomena in a new light' (Robson, 1993; Saunders et al, 2000). The objective of this type of research is to shed light on a previously unexplored area or issues. Descriptive research serves 'to portray an accurate profile of persons, events or situations' (Robson, 1993). The objective of this type of research is to obtain a clear picture of what happens. It may be an extension of, or a forerunner to, a piece of exploratory research (Saunders et al, 2000). Explanatory research is aimed at explaining why things happen. The objective of this type of research is to establish and explain causal relationships between variables (Cooper and Emory, 1995; Saunders et al., 2000).

The purpose of research can be further clarified by the type of research questions posed. Exploratory research generally deals with 'how' and 'what' questions. Descriptive research is concerned with finding out the answers to 'how many'/'how much', 'when', 'where', 'who' questions. Explanatory research is normally characterized by 'why' questions (Robson, 1993; Cooper and Emory, 1995; Saunders et al., 2000).

Three conditions usually have to be considered when selecting a research strategy for a particular research project (Yin, 2003). These three conditions consist of (a) the type of research question posed, (b) the extent of control that an investigator has over actual behavioural events, and (c) the degree of focus on contemporary phenomena as opposed to historical events. Table 4.3 shows how each of the three conditions is related to the five major research strategies (Yin, 2003).

Table 4.3   An overview of research strategies

Strategy	Form of research question	Requires control of behavioural events?	Focuses on contemporary events?
Experiment	how, why?	Yes	Yes
Survey	who,what,where,how many,how much?	No	Yes
Archival analysis	who,what,where,how many,how much?	No	Yes/No
History	how,why?	No	No
Case study	how,why?	No	Yes

Knowledge management is a relatively new research area. Knowledge management only emerged as an explicit area of pursuit for managing organizations and as a topic of serious study or academic knowledge transfer in 1990s (Wiig, 1997; Sveiby, 1997; Wenger, 1998; Earl, 2001). The concept of knowledge management is still in its infancy (Davenport and Prusak, 2000). As such, inquiries into knowledge management are most likely to fall into the domain of explorative research.

This study focuses in particular on the role of ICT in support of knowledge management. Even though many knowledge management initiatives use ICT, there are few well-established models or frameworks to explain the impacting factors and provide guidelines for knowledge management practice. This further justifies the exploratory nature of this study with the use of 'what' and 'how' types of questions. The study obviously deals with contemporary events in that knowledge management became a matter of concern to organizations only a decade or so ago (Wiig, 1997; Sveiby, 1997). In such a situation, issues related to archival analysis are excluded for this study. Since there has been only a limited access to and control of actual behavioural events in this study, experiment was not an appropriate method in that it requires manipulating behaviour directly, precisely and systematically (Yin, 2003).

Subject to the resources available to this study, some other options such as those of ethnography and action research were not adopted. Ethnography is very time-consuming (Saunders et al., 2000). This study had to be completed in a given time frame. Action research requires the involvement of practitioners in the research. This was not an option for this study.

The discussion above suggests that survey and case study methods are appropriate for this study within the constraints of the time and resources available. Survey is a quantitative method, which can collect a large amount of data from a sizeable population in a highly economical way and caters for the 'what?' and 'how?' questions (Saunders et al., 2000). Case study is a qualitative method, which can gain a rich understanding of the context and the process of implementing knowledge management projects. The combination of quantitative and qualitative research conforms to the choice of the research philosophy, the research approach and the time horizon for this study. It enables triangulation and enhances the robustness and rigorousness of the research. Chapter 5 discusses in detail the methods of data collection in this study.

4.3 A hybrid research approach

Figure 4.2 shows a hybrid research approach adopted in this study. It combines quantitative and qualitative methods as discussed above. The multi-method approach allows the research to exploit the advantages of individual methods and minimize the negative effects that different methods might have on the research results. It is quite common for a single study to combine quantitative and qualitative methods and to use primary and secondary data (Saunders et al., 2000).

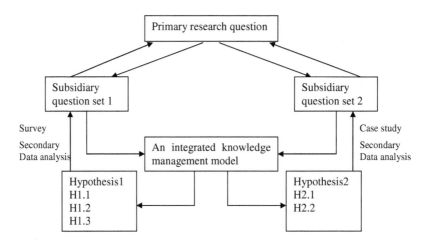

Figure 4.2   The hybrid research approach

The quantitative research in this study employs a survey method. The major strengths of survey include its versatility, its efficiency and its economy (Bryman and Bell, 2003). The major weakness of adopting such a method is that the quality of information secured depends heavily on the ability and willingness of respondents to cooperate. It also requires much time spent on designing and piloting the questionnaire and analyzing the result (Saunders et al., 2000).

This study employs a survey in order to investigate the conversion processes between information and knowledge in the context of organizational knowledge management. The distinction between information and knowledge is often treated theoretically. However, there has been little empirical research into the conversion processes between information and knowledge. To explore the mechanisms that facilitate the conversion between information and knowledge, 'what' and 'how' types of questions are posed. A survey is suitable for asking exploratory questions. It can provide a broad picture of respondents' experiences and impacting factors in the conversion processes between information and knowledge.

However, a survey also has its limitations as mentioned above. To minimize these limitations and to ensure the reliability and validity of the research findings, the survey instrument, data collection and analysis should be carefully designed and conducted (Bryman and Bell, 2003; Yin, 2003). This includes survey questionnaire design, the criteria for and selection of targeted respondents, conduct of a pilot survey, delivery, data collection, and data analysis. Chapter 5 presents a comprehensive discussion on these issues.

The qualitative research in this study employs case study to gain a rich understanding of the context and the process of implementing knowledge management projects. To ensure the reliability and validity of the research findings, careful attention must be given to the case selection process, the design of interview questions, interviewee selection, data collection, and data analysis. Chapter 5 covers these issues.

4.4 Concluding remarks

A research methodology is concerned with how to answer a set of research questions and how to meet the research objectives. The selection of the research methodology for this study is based on the research process 'onion' and conforms to the choice of underlying research philosophy, research strategy adopted and time horizon. A mixture of quantitative and qualitative techniques is employed for this study.

The quantitative research element adopts a survey to investigate the use of electronic resources for a better understanding of the conversion process between information and knowledge. It is used to investigate users' experience, perception and opinions about the use of electronic resources at individual level.

The qualitative research dimension adopts the case study method to gain a richer understanding of the factors influencing current knowledge management practice and the implementation of knowledge management projects. Case studies combine primary and secondary data collection and analysis.

Chapter 5

Research Design and Implementation

5.1   Introduction

Once an appropriate research methodology has been chosen, the emphasis of the research shifts to the design and implementation of research instruments in order to ensure the validity and reliability of the research findings (Robson, 1993; Cooper and Emory, 1995; Saunders et al., 2000; Yin, 2003). Measures have to be taken to design and conduct the questionnaire survey and case study for the hybrid approach using a combination of quantitative and qualitative research methods.

The research design constitutes the blueprint for the collection, measurement, and analysis of data (Cooper and Emory, 1995). It involves (a) selecting sources and types of information used to answer the research questions; (b) specifying the relationships among the study's variables; and (c) outlining each procedure for conduct of the research. The research design not only provides the plan and structure for an investigator to obtain answers to research questions, but also helps researchers to allocate their limited resources in order to complete the research project within time and financial constraints (Robson, 1993; Cooper and Emory, 1995).

However, unless the research project is conducted appropriately, a well-design research project will not necessarily result in valid research findings. The research must be implemented in such a manner that the findings of the research can be validated (Bryman and Bell, 2003; Yin, 2003). Proper implementation will lead to greater confidence in the validity and reliability of the research findings.

This chapter presents the design and implementation of the research for this study. It first discusses the design and development of the questionnaire including the design of the survey, the selection of the survey sample, the procedures for conducting the survey, the collection of data, the analysis of the survey data, the validity and reliability of the survey results, and the ethical issues involved in the conduct of the survey. After discussion of the survey design and development, the chapter describes the design and implementation of the qualitative research method. This includes the selection of the case, the collection of secondary data, and the analysis of collected data. It also includes the design of interview questions and the collection of primary data in the case study. The chapter finishes with a discussion on the analysis of the data, the validity and reliability of the research findings, and the ethical issues involved in the case study.

5.2 The design and implementation of a survey

5.2.1 The development of the questionnaire

Questionnaires are structured instruments. They are an effective means to gather data from a potentially large number of respondents (Bryman and Bell, 2003; Yin, 2003). A well-designed questionnaire can gather both overall and specific opinions, experiences, and attitudes on a specific research topic.

In the knowledge object conversion model, the conversion processes between information and knowledge is the most elusive. This is because there is no clear distinction between these two components (Tuomi, 2000; Song et al., 2003; Spiegler, 2003). To help understand the role of ICT in the conversion of information and knowledge in knowledge management, three dimensions of purpose, user and value were proposed. These dimensions and other impacting factors in the conversion of information and knowledge formed the main contents of the questionnaire.

With the pervasive application of web technology and the Internet, electronic resources are readily available and accessible. They include journals, newspapers, archives, theses, government papers and other materials in electronic form. The electronic resources have become important information resources for individuals (Gandhi, 2004). To gain knowledge from the use of electronic resources is not uncommon. As such, the questionnaire survey has chosen electronic resources as a vehicle for better understanding the transformation between information and knowledge.

The survey was designed to investigate the experience of individuals in the use of electronic resources provided by a university library. Through the survey, the main factors influencing the conversion processes between information and knowledge could be identified, and the dimensions along the conversion processes could be tested.

Hence, the unit of analysis was the individual user of electronic resources. The content of the questionnaire was divided into four sections as follows:
- Background
- Use of Electronic Resources
- Role of Electronic Resources
- Impacting Factors

Appendix A includes the questionnaire developed to identify the use of electronic resources. Section 1 was designed to identify the user profile including job position, tenure, education level, age, and gender. Section 2 was designed to investigate the experience, access location, access content, access frequency, the purpose, the reason for access, and any prior training in using the electronic resources. These data were collected to test the user and purpose dimensions in the conversion processes between information and knowledge. Section 3 was designed to investigate information demand, knowledge input, knowledge integration, value, and purpose. These data were collected to test the user and purpose and value dimensions in the conversion processes between information and knowledge.

Section 4 was designed to investigate the impacting factors in the conversion processes between information and knowledge. The respondents were required to indicate the degree to which they agreed or disagreed with ten statements. These statements included factors such as information relevance, information overload, information update, time consumption, support equipment, accessibility, training, help/instruction, example/experience exploitation, and information 'push'. Considering that there might be more impacting factors, open-ended questions were included to accommodate broader concerns.

Although the questionnaire survey was designed to target the users of electronic resources, not all the respondents might happen to have experience in using electronic resources. Therefore, the questionnaire was also designed to cover these respondents.

5.2.2 Targeted respondents

The targeted respondents were individual users of electronic resources in a university environment. The exact total population was unknown because the university library did not provide any avenue to identify the users of electronic resources. Considering that all staff and students in the university could access electronic resources, all staff and students were potential respondents. At the time of the questionnaire distribution, there were around 3360 full-time staff and 56,000 students in the university involved in the survey (University annual report, 2005). However, the user population of electronic resources would be expected to be much smaller.

5.2.3 Delivery of the questionnaire

The survey was conducted online. The advantages of online surveys include the widespread reach to potential respondents, low cost, potential for quick response, computerised data formats, and ability to monitor the response process (Saunders et al, 2000; Ticehurst and Veal, 2000; Bryman and Bell, 2003). They also offer the capacity to arrange the layout of the questionnaire in many ways. The checkbox and option box can allow respondents to make multiple choices or a single choice where necessary. In this way, the likelihood of response errors can be reduced. The flexible text box enables respondents to type as many words as they wish, which is not the case with printed questionnaires.

After the questionnaire was mounted on a web site, it was piloted to test its layout, the wording of questions, the sequencing of questions, the Likert-scale responses, the route of skipping some questions, introductory remarks, the hyperlink, and the result of submission. According to the results of the pilot survey, some necessary revisions to the questionnaire were made.

The key to successful surveys (online or hard copy) is to reach the potential respondents and to maximize the responses. Since the survey was exploratory, it was difficult to identify members of the desired population. Self-selection is an option to find the desired respondents. There are two ways to reach potential respondents. One is to put the hyperlink of the online survey on the website of the electronic resources. The users of the electronic resources would then see it and might complete the survey. However in this case, this was not an option owing to space limitations on the electronic resources website. The other way is to invite potential respondents to participate via email. As massive emails and spam emails have been increasing and annoying email recipients, the response rate to this approach could be really low. The use of authorized email lists to distribute the letter of invitation to participate could be a safer way of increasing the participation rate.

After negotiating access to authorized email lists, it was found that weekly staff electronic newsletters and fortnightly student electronic newsletters were an appropriate channel for the distribution of the letter of invitation. The content of the newsletters is on a website and the table of contents of newsletters is sent via email lists. If recipients are interested in specific content, they can hit the hyperlink of the newsletter website and browse that content. The average 'hit' of these two newsletters indicate that about two-thirds of staff and about 7% of students access the newsletters. To supplement this channel, some course email lists were utilized and an invitation message was also published in the 'Library News' and the 'Student Learning Hub News'. Individuals were able to indicate their willingness to take part in the survey. In such circumstances, the respondents self-selected themselves and were most likely the users of electronic resources.

5.2.4 Data collection

The online survey was designed and conducted for self-administered completion and self-submission by the respondents. The submitted survey results were saved directly into a computerised file, which could be downloaded anytime during the process of the survey and readily used in any data analysis software package. This sped up the data collection and analysis process considerably, and cut down the possibility of error in transcribing results from questionnaire to computer. In the meantime, each response was also sent to the investigator via email for monitoring of the process.

5.2.5 Data analysis

The Statistical Packages for Social Sciences (SPSS) v12.0.1 for Windows was used to analyse the online survey data. Following the survey data analysis procedure shown in Figure 5.1, the first step was to prepare the data for analysis. After importing the CSV-format file into SPSS, variables were defined for each of the single-choice questions. Any respondent could tick all the boxes of the multiple-choice questions, so each of them had to be a separate variable.

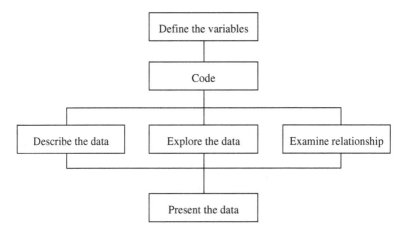

Figure 5.1   The procedure for analyzing survey data

In addition to defining the variables, the results of the questionnaire responses had to be converted into numerical codes. For multiple-choice questions, each option was treated as a single variable with '1' indicating 'selected' and '0' indicating 'not selected'. Five-point Likert-scale responses were used to code the attitude statements of impacting factors, ranging from '1' indicating 'strongly agree' to '5' indicating 'strongly disagree'. Similarly, Five-point Likert-scale responses were applied to code the usefulness of electronic resources with '1' indicating 'extremely useful' and '5' indicating 'not useful'. For categorical variables, a whole number was assigned to each category. For example, the age of a respondent fell into any of six categories, with '1' assigned to the category of 'less than 20' and '6' to the category of '60 and over'.

A few submissions were found to have missing responses to individual questions. These missing data were replaced with mean values during the course of data analysis.

The survey data were analyzed using descriptive statistics to obtain a demographic snapshot of respondents. This was principally achieved by a frequencies and means analysis of the data in section 1 of the questionnaire. Survey data were explored by comparing their specific value and interdependence, highest and lowest values, totals, proportions, and distributions. Cross-tabulation analysis was employed to identify the relationship among the user, purpose and value dimensions. Graphics and tables were used to present the data.

5.2.6   Validity and reliability of the research findings

In order to ensure the validity and reliability of the survey, the process of questionnaire construction, survey piloting, survey delivering, data collection, and data analysis had to be carefully designed and implemented.

Validity is the extent to which the data collected truly reflect the phenomena being studied (Ticehurst and Veal, 2000). It is concerned with collection of the correct data for the research objectives. The questions in the questionnaire must reflect this concern. On the other hand, reliability is the extent to which research findings would be the same if the research were to be repeated at a later date, or with a different sample of subjects (Ticehurst and Veal, 2000). It is concerned with stability, equivalence, internal consistency, and reproducibility (Cooper and Emory, 1995; Corbetta, 2003).

Neuman (1994) suggests four principles to enhance reliability and validity: (a) clearly conceptualized constructs, (b) use of a precise level of measurement, (c) use of multiple indicators and (d) use of pilot tests. The questions designed for the questionnaire were asked in a straightforward and unambiguous manner. This follows the first principle and avoids the possibility of different interpretations by respondents. The second principle was achieved by assigning a five-point scale to attitude statements and whole numbers to the categorical measures. The third principle was observed by including more than one question to indicate the different aspects of the same dimension and asking essentially the same thing in different parts of the questionnaire (Ticehurst and Veal, 2000). For example, in section 2 of the questionnaire, a question was designed to ask respondents the purpose of using electronic resource, while later in section 3, respondents were asked to name the situation where electronic resources are useful. The responses of these two questions could be tested for consistency.

The pilot survey was conducted before the distribution of the letter of invitation via email and news bulletin. Seven participants including staff and students tested the survey layout, the wording of questions, the sequencing of questions, the measurement of questions, the completion time, the introductory remarks, the hyperlink, and the submission process. Based on feedback from the pilot test, some revisions to the questionnaire were made to enhance its validity and reliability.

5.2.7 Ethical issues

Ethical issues arise when research involves human subjects (Ticehurst and Veal, 2000). The online survey was subject to and adhered to the Ethics Policy and Procedures of RMIT University. Privacy, confidentiality, anonymity, freedom of choice to participate in the survey and to withdraw the unprocessed data were guaranteed in the design and conduct of the online survey, and in the reporting of results. The potential respondents were informed through the letter of invitation and the introductory remarks of the questionnaire.

5.3 The design and implementation of secondary data analysis

Secondary data are the data that have already been collected for some other purposes (Hakim, 1982). The advantages of using secondary data include fewer resource requirements (Ghauri et al., 1995), higher-quality data (Stewart and Kamins, 1993), unobtrusiveness (Stewart and Kamins, 1993), serendipitous discovery (Dale et al. 1988), and permanence of data (Denscomebe, 1998). These data can be used to help to triangulate findings based on other data such as documents and primary data collected through observation, interviews or questionnaires (Saunders et al., 2000). By analyzing a variety of published secondary data, the critical success factors in implementation of knowledge management projects can be identified and compared with the results of primary data analysis. Secondary data also provide the possibility of access to a wide range of case studies covering the different projects in different industries and regions.

The main disadvantage of using secondary data is that they have been collected for a specific purpose (Denscomebe, 1998) and may not be suitable for helping to answer the research questions or may only be able to support partial findings. As such, secondary data must be carefully assessed and evaluated.

The overall and precise suitability of secondary data was assessed including measurement validity, coverage and unmeasured variables and the source of the data. The costs and benefits of using secondary data were also assessed.

The collection of secondary data involves two steps. The first step is to ascertain whether the data are available and the second step is to locate the precise data required. Since 1998, the KNOW Network has announced the 20 Global Most Admired Knowledge Enterprises (MAKE) winners based on eight key knowledge performance dimensions each year. So far, 48 organizations have been recognized as Global MAKE Winners. These organizations are actively engaged in knowledge management projects and they can be regarded as representing best practice in knowledge management. Their achievements have been published as case studies on websites, in journals, magazines, conference proceedings and other sources. These enabled the collection of cases for investigation of critical success factors in the implementation of knowledge management projects.

The unit of analysis in these case studies was the knowledge management project and the focus was on the ICT in support of knowledge management processes and the conversion processes of knowledge objects. The secondary data analysis was carried out following the procedures described in the following section.

5.4   The design and implementation of a case study

5.4.1   Case selection

A field case was chosen to further explore the factors influencing the implementation of a knowledge management project and to validate the findings drawn from the case studies obtained from the secondary data. The case involved the pilot implementation of a knowledge portal designed to centralize file storage and sharing for the Program Quality Management System (PQMS) at four departments in a university.

In this field case study, multiple data collection techniques were employed as a strategy of triangulation (Eisenhardt 1989; Denscombe 1998). These included unstructured and semi-structured interviews with project team members and users involved in the implementation of the knowledge portal, observations made during the meetings, visits to the websites, and documentation reviews. The interviews were mainly conducted face-to-face, supplemented by telephone and email. The interviewees were selected to reflect different roles in the implementation of the knowledge portal. The interview questions were designed according to these different roles. The field case study was conducted in two stages.

The first stage was to explore the context and background in which the knowledge portal was initiated. To this end, the opening interviews were much less structured. Each interview lasted for between 30-120 minutes. The period of data collection for this in-depth case study was one year (June 2004-June 2005), in which three unstructured interviews and observations of three project meetings were carried out. During this period of time, the relevant documents were collected, the websites were accessed, the main events were observed and interviewees for the semi-structured interview were identified.

The second stage was to conduct the semi-structured interviews. The period of data collection for these semi-structured interviews was from June 2005 to October 2005. Twelve interviews were carried out. Each interview lasted for between 30 – 60 minutes and was recorded. After each interview, the recorded information was transcribed into document form for analysis.

5.4.2 Qualitative data analysis

After empirical data were collected from multiple sources, the data analysis was carried out following the procedures shown in Figure 5.2:

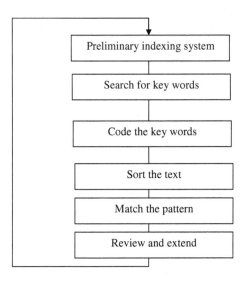

Figure 5.2   The procedure for analyzing case study data

A preliminary indexing system was established based on the literature review and research questions. Then from the text of empirical materials, searches of key words or phrases were conducted, and coded according to the preliminary indexing system. Particular pieces of text and associated ideas were sorted using the preliminary indexing system. Notes were made to match the emerging patterns, relationships and recurring themes and the preliminary indexing system was reviewed and extended. If there was any ambiguity or any incomplete information, follow-ups were then made through telephone, email or face-to-face interviews. This resulted in further data collection and analysis with the whole process operating in a recursive fashion.

5.4.3 Validity and reliability of the research findings

To increase the quality of case studies, Yin (2003) suggests some tactics for construct validity, internal validity, external validity, and reliability. These tactics are shown in Table 5.1 (Yin, 2003).

Table 5.1   Tactics for four design tests in case study

Tests	Tactics	Research Phases
Construct validity	Use multiple sources of evidence	Data collection
	Establish chain of evidence	Data collection
	Review draft report by key informants	Composition
Internal validity	Do pattern-matching	Data analysis
	Do explanation-building	Data analysis
	Address rival explanations	Data analysis
	Use logic models	Data analysis
External validity	Use theory in single-case studies	Research design
	Use replication logic in multiple-case studies	Research design
Reliability	Use case study protocol	Data collection
	Develop case study database	Data collection

These tactics were adopted in the different phases to ensure the validity and reliability of the case studies conducted. In the research design phase, the theoretical research framework was used to select the cases. The knowledge portal was applied in the different departments, enabling replication to take place.

In the data collection phase, multiple types of evidence were collected from books, journals, magazines, documents, meeting minutes, interviews, websites and observations. A plan for conducting the case study served as the protocol including an overview of the case, data collection procedures, and case study questions.

In the data analysis phase, pattern-matching, explanation-building and logic models were used and conflicting explanations were addressed.

5.4.4 Ethical issues in case study

Ethical issues also arose in the conduct of the case study, especially in the conduct of the semi-structured interviews. The interviews were subject to and adhered to the Ethics Policy and Procedures of RMIT University. The privacy, confidentiality, anonymity, freedom of choice to participate in the interviews and to withdraw the unprocessed data were guaranteed during the conduct of the interviews, and in the reporting of results. The interviewees were informed prior to the interview and consent was obtained from each interviewee.

5. 5 Concluding remarks

The quantitative research method in this study employed an online questionnaire survey to investigate the use of electronic resources for the better understanding of the conversion processes between information and knowledge. The survey was used to investigate users' experiences, perceptions and opinions relating to the use of electronic resources at an individual level. In order to maximize the validity and reliability of the survey, careful attention was paid to the questionnaire design, sample selection, survey procedure, data collection and data analysis.

The qualitative research method in this study employed a case study approach to gain a richer understanding of the factors influencing current knowledge management practice and the implementation of knowledge management projects. The case studies combined primary and secondary data collection and analysis. To ensure the validity and reliability of the case study, measures were taken to ensure that design of interview questions, case selection, the case study procedures, data collection of primary and secondary cases, and data analysis all conformed to research best practice.

Chapter 6

Conversion between Information and

Knowledge: an Analysis of the Survey

6.1 Introduction

In the fast changing economic and organizational climate, individuals and organizations are increasingly aware of the need to create new knowledge, identify, value, and evolve their knowledge from the vast range of information resources available. Individual knowledge generated contributes further into the pool of information resources, resulting in the development and creation of more knowledge. Organizations strive to turn individual knowledge into organizational knowledge and make the most out of it (Wolford and Kwiecien, 2003).

The rapid advance of ICT provides an unprecedented opportunity to access and search for much broader sources of information in a much faster manner and at much cheaper cost (Adams and Bonk, 1995; Klobas, 1997; Stromquist and Samoff, 2000; Lueg, 2001). The application of ICT offers the potential for faster and cheaper means of communication that could greatly facilitate organizational knowledge sharing. The widespread availability and adoption of ICT have offered tremendous possibilities for constructing, acquiring, storing and representing knowledge (Jackson, 1999). The use of ICT provides new means of interactivity and association, facilitating the process of conversion between information and knowledge. This research project starts from the premise that for knowledge management to be effective, this conversion process must be understood.

This study investigates the use of electronic resources as a means of shedding light on the conversion processes between information and knowledge for effective organizational knowledge management. The rapid advance of ICT, especially the advent of web technology, has made electronic resources readily available and easily accessible (Adams and Bonk, 1995; Klobas, 1997; Stromquist and Samoff, 2000; Lueg, 2001). Technological developments offer unprecedented opportunities to access electronic resources and retrieve information and knowledge.

Electronic resources cover databases, books, journals, newspapers, magazines, archives, theses, conference papers, examination papers, government papers, research reports, scripts and monographs in electronic form (Rehman and Ramzy, 2004). In contrast with accessing the printed counterpart, the benefits of using electronic resources include (a) accessing sources in a timely manner; (b) accessing them free of time, stock, and space constraints; (c) the richness and wide variety of resources available; and (d) the ease of search through search engines (Rehman and Ramzy, 2004). These benefits attract more investment in the collections of electronic resources, resulting in their significant growth (Zhang and Haslam, 2005). Electronic resources are a valuable element of information resources widely searched and explored by users (Liew and Foo, 1999).

This investigation of the use of electronic resources will not only increase understanding of the conversion processes between information and knowledge, and of the role of ICT in these conversion processes, but also will provide new insights into the field of knowledge management. To fully appreciate the role of ICT in the use of electronic resources, an online questionnaire survey was designed as discussed in Chapter 5 to investigate the use of electronic resources in a university environment.

This chapter presents and discusses the results of the online survey. It first shows the demographic characteristics of respondents from the data collected in the survey, followed by an examination of the use patterns of electronic resources. The chapter then discusses the role of electronic resources in the processes of conversion between information and knowledge. The main factors which affect the use of electronic resources are summarized. The chapter finishes with a discussion of the correlations among three dimensions of the use of electronic resources, the validity and reliability of the survey results, and the implications of the survey results in effective knowledge management.

6.2 Demographic characteristics

The online survey attracted 317 responses, some of which were duplicates or invalid on the grounds of incomplete submission. After removing these repeat and invalid submissions, 305 valid responses remained for further analysis. In the remaining data, a few submissions were found to have missing responses to individual questions. These missing data were replaced with mean values during the course of data analysis.

The profile of the respondents is reflected in their job position, number of years in their current position, their level of education, age, and gender. Most of the 305 respondents were females (55.7%), in the age group of 20 to 29 years (36.7%), and in their current position less than 5 years (82.3%). A majority of the respondents had university degrees (72.5%), with the rest having a TAFE-level and high school education. They included postgraduate students (39%), undergraduate students (38%), academic staff (13.1%), administrative staff (8.5%), and TAFE students (1.3%). Table 6.1 shows the demographic characteristics of the respondents in terms of position, tenure, age, education background, and gender.

Table 6.1   Profile of respondents

Profile		Frequency	Percent
Position group	TAFE Student	4	1.3%
	Undergraduate Student	116	38.0%
	Postgraduate Student by Coursework	68	22.3%
	Postgraduate Student by Research	51	16.7%
	Administrative Staff	26	8.5%
	Academic Staff	40	13.1%
Years in current position	Less than 1 year	105	34.4%
	1-4 years	146	47.9%
	5-10 years	37	12.1%
	11-25 years	13	4.3%
	More than 25 years	4	1.3%
Education background	High School	39	12.8%
	TAFE	45	14.8%
	Undergraduate	117	38.4%
	Postgraduate	79	25.9%
	PhD or equivalent	25	8.2%
Age group	<20	48	15.7%
	20-29	112	36.7%
	30-39	66	21.6%
	40-49	39	12.8%
	50-59	34	11.1%
	>60	6	2.0%
Gender group	Female	170	55.7%
	Male	135	44.3%

6.3   Use patterns of electronic resources

The use patterns of electronic resources are highly relevant to the investigation of the role of ICT for effective knowledge management. In the current study, only 12 out 305 respondents had not used electronic resources. Figure 6.1 shows the proportion of users and non-users among all the respondents. This suggests that electronic resources are vital to teaching, learning and research in universities today.

Figure 6.1   A comparison of users and non-users of electronic resources

The frequency of use of electronic resources is also interesting in this study. With the data collected, 180 respondents out of 305 respondents were found to have used electronic resources more than once a week. Figure 6.2 demonstrates the frequency of the use of electronic resources.

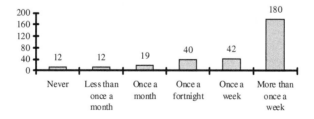

Figure 6.2   A profile of the use of electronic resources

With regard to the location for accessing electronic resources, users were able to access electronic resources at a range of locations. In the survey, these locations were grouped into four categories: (a) within the library; (b) outside the library and on the campus; (c) onshore and off the campus, and (d) offshore and off the campus. Table 6.2 shows the frequency and percent of respondents accessing electronic resources compared with those who did not access electronic resources in the same category of location. It was found that the highest percent (66.9%) of respondents accessed electronic resources onshore and off the campus, indicating that users were not restrained by physical space limitations.

Table 6.2   An overview of accessing locations

Locations	Response	Frequency	Percent
Off campus and onshore	Yes	204	66.9
	No	101	33.1
On campus and outside the library	Yes	181	59.3
	No	124	40.7
Within the library	Yes	150	49.2
	No	155	50.8
Off campus and offshore	Yes	38	12.5
	No	267	87.5

Users were able to access electronic resources not only from a single category of location, but also from multiple categories of location mentioned above. Table 6.3 shows the frequency and percent of respondents accessing electronic resources from a single category of location and from multiple categories of locations. It was found that 61.4% of respondents accessed them at a multiple categories of locations including the library, outside the library, and off the campus, free of physical space constraints. This is supplemented by comments from respondents at home, overseas, in distance learning mode and those who were disabled. With the use of ICT, it is possible to access the electronic resources without the constraints of time and location.

Table 6.3   A comparison between single and multiple location of access

Locations of Access	Frequency	Percent
No access	14	4.6%
Single category of location	104	34.1%
Combination of two categories of locations	106	34.8%
Combination of three categories of locations	67	22.0%
Combination of four categories of locations	14	4.6%

Since multiple responses were allowed to the location of access question, the frequency analysis for the multiple responses is shown in Table 6.4. It shows that accessing electronic resources took place most off campus onshore (35.6% of all responses to the location), followed with on campus outside the library (31.6%), on campus in the library (26.2%), and off campus offshore (6.6%).

Table 6.4   A multiple location access profile

Locations	Count	Percent of Responses	Percent of Respondents
Off campus and onshore	204	35.6%	70.1%
On campus and outside the library	181	31.6%	62.2%
Within the library	150	26.2%	51.5%
Off campus and offshore	38	6.6%	13.1%
Total responses	573	100.0%	196.9%

In regard to what types of electronic resources users accessed, the survey listed nine categories of electronic resources: (a) library catalogue; (b) online journals; (c) website information; (d) online newspapers; (e) electronic books; (f) online magazines; (g) online archives; (h) online theses; and (i) exam papers. Table 6.5 presents the frequency and percent of categories of electronic resources accessed by respondents. Amongst these different categories of electronic resources, it was found that highest percent (82%) of respondents used the library catalogue compared with respondents who did not use the same category of resource.

Table 6.5   A classification of electronic resources

Categories of Electronic Resources	Frequency	Percent
Library catalogue	250	82.0%
Online journals	235	77.0%
Website information	208	68.2%
Online newspapers	151	49.5%
Electronic books	93	30.5%
Online magazines	92	30.2%
Online archives	68	22.3%
Online theses	63	20.7%
Electronic exam papers	58	19.0%

Users often accessed more than one category of electronic resources. Therefore, multiple responses were allowed to the question of the categories of electronic resources accessed by the respondents. There were 1218 responses given by 305 respondents, indicating many respondents accessed multiple categories of electronic resources. Table 6.6 shows a further inspection of frequency analysis for the multiple responses. It is evident that the library catalogue, online journals, website information, and online newspapers were the most popular resources. Their proportions among all the responses were 20.5%, 19.3%, 17.1% and 12.4% respectively.

Table 6.6   A classification of electronic resources (multiple responses)

Categories of Electronic Resources	Count	Percent of Responses	Percent of Respondents
Library catalogue	250	20.5%	85.6%
Online journals	235	19.3%	80.5%
Website information	208	17.1%	71.2%
Online newspapers	151	12.4%	51.7%
Electronic books	93	7.6%	31.8%
Online magazines	92	7.6%	31.5%
Online archives	8	5.6%	23.3%
Online theses	63	5.2%	21.6%
Electronic exam paper	58	4.8%	19.9%
Total responses	1218	100.0%	417.1%

Users accessed electronic sources for different purposes. These purposes were (a) to gather information on a specific topic; (b) to gain general information; (c) to get answers to specific questions; (d) to complete assignments; (e) to review literature; (f) to write essays; and (g) to make decisions. Table 6.7 presents the frequency and percent of users accessing electronic resources for each purpose. It was found that the highest percent (82.3%) of respondents accessed electronic resources in order to gather information on a specific topic and the lowest percent (25.2%) of respondents accessed electronic resources for the purpose of making a decision.

Table 6.7   The purposes for accessing electronic resources

Purposes of Accessing Electronic Resources	Frequency	Percent
To gather information on a specific topic	251	82.3%
To gain general information	214	70.2%
To get answers to specific questions	212	69.5%
To complete an assignment	169	55.4%
To do a literature review	153	50.2%
To write an essay	129	42.3%
To make a decision	77	25.2%

The purpose of using electronic resources could be diverse. Therefore, respondents were allowed to give multiple choices for their purposes to access electronic resources. Accordingly, multiple responses were grouped for the frequency analysis. There were 1205 responses to the purposes of using electronic resources given by 305 respondents. Table 6.8 shows the frequency and percent of responses to the purposes of using electronic resources. Of all the possible purposes, to gather information on a specific topic, to gain general information and to get answers to specific questions were the most common. Their percentages of all the responses were 20.8%, 17.8% and 17.6% respectively.

Table 6.8   **The purposes for accessing electronic resources**

(Multiple responses)

Purposes of accessing electronic resources	Count	Percent of Responses	Percent of respondents
To gather information on a specific topic	251	20.8%	85.7%
To gain general information	214	17.8%	73.0%
To get answers to specific questions	212	17.6%	72.4%
To complete an assignment	169	14.0%	57.7%
To do a literature review	153	12.7%	52.2%
To write an essay	129	10.7%	44.0%
To make a decision	77	6.4%	26.3%
Total responses	1205	100.0%	411.3%

There were clear advantages from accessing electronic resources (Rehman and Ramzy, 2004). Those advantages were the main reasons why users accessed electronic resources. Five main reasons were listed in the survey including: (a) the ease of access; (b) time saving; (c) wide variety of resources available; (d) availability of search tools; and (e) no physical space limitation.

Table 6.9 shows the frequency and percent of respondents accessing electronic resources for each reason. It was found that the highest percent (86.2%) of respondents thought that 'ease of access' was a reason for using electronic resources. Respondents were also allowed to give other reasons for their use of electronic resources. Other reasons were 'quality of information', 'the only source available' or 'a compulsory requirement.'

Table 6.9 Main reasons for accessing electronic resources

Reasons of Accessing Electronic Resources	Frequency	Percent
Easy to access	263	86.2%
Saves time	223	73.1%
Wide variety of resources available	221	72.5%
Availability of search tools	165	54.1%
There are no physical space limitations	124	40.7%

Likewise, users might access electronic resources for different reasons. Therefore, respondents were allowed to have multiple choices for their reason to use electronic resources. There were 996 responses to the reasons of using electronic resources. Table 6.10 shows the frequency and percent of responses to each reason. Of all possible main reasons for using electronic resources, ease of access was the most popular with a 26.4% response rate.

Table 6.10 Main reasons for accessing electronic resources
(Multiple responses)

Purposes of Accessing Electronic Resources	Count	Percent of Responses	Percent of Respondents
Easy to access	263	26.4%	92.0%
Saves time	223	22.4%	78.0%
Wide variety available	221	22.2%	77.3%
Availability of search tools	165	16.6%	57.7%
No physical space limitations	124	12.4%	43.4%
Total responses	996	100.0%	348.3%

About half the respondents (50.2%) had not undertaken any training in the use of electronic resources. Figure 6.3 shows the proportion of respondents with training and without training.

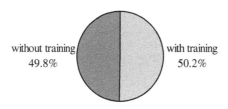

without training
49.8%

with training
50.2%

Figure 6.3   A comparison of users with training and without training

6.4   The   role   of   electronic   resources   in   knowledge management

Electronic resources are readily available and easily accessible. However, the value of electronic resources is realized through the active interaction between users and electronic resources (Liew and Foo, 1999). Users access, absorb, digest and apply electronic resources in their work or study makes electronic resources valuable. As electronic resources are important in support of problem solving and decision making, it is important to investigate where they have been used and the perceived value resulting from use.

The use of electronic resources was essential for the majority of respondents in this survey. Table 6.11 shows that 87.9% of respondents said that using electronic resources formed part of their work/study and 70.8% of respondents had integrated electronic resources into the tasks undertaken. Even though 43.9% of respondents had made their ideas available electronically, publishing any item of scholarship in electronic form was relatively low in the proportion, with 19.7% of the respondents having done so.

Table 6.11   The role of electronic resources

Role of Electronic Resources in the Work/Study		Frequency	Percent
The use of electronic resources is part of work/study	Yes	268	87.9%
	Intend to	4	1.3%
	No	20	6.6%
	Non users	13	4.3%
Integrate electronic resources into any task undertaken	Yes	216	70.8%
	Intend to	18	5.9%
	No	57	18.7%
	Non users	14	4.6%
Make the ideas available electronically	Yes	134	43.9%
	Intend to	33	10.8%
	No	124	40.7%
	Non users	14	4.6%
Publish electronically	Yes	60	19.7%
	Intend to	30	9.8%
	No	203	66.6%
	Non users	12	3.9%

Therefore, it is not surprising that 55.1% of respondents believed that electronic resources were extremely useful, 31.8% of respondents believed they were quite useful, and 6.6% of respondents thought they were useful. Figure 6.4 shows the numbers of respondents responding to the scale of the usefulness of electronic resources.

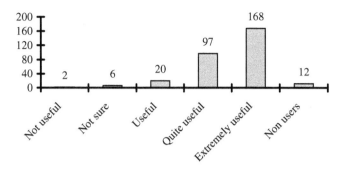

Figure 6.4   The usefulness of electronic resources

Respondents were asked about the situations where they have used electronic resources and when they thought electronic resources were useful. These situations included (a) in completing some a written task work; (b) in undertaking a research project; (c) in gaining new ideas; (d) in comparing different views; (e) in undertaking a new task; (f) in making a complex decision; (g) in undertaking a routine task, and (h) in making a simple decision. Of all these situations, respondents said that electronic resources were most useful in a situation where some writing had to be completed, with the highest percent (77.4%) of respondents choosing this situation compared to those who did not choose it. Table 6.12 shows the frequency and percentage of responses to each situation using electronic resources.

Electronic resources could be used in different situations. Users were allowed to have multiple choices to the situations where they accessed electronic resources. Multiple responses analysis was therefore undertaken to test for consistency with the above results. Table 6.13 shows the frequency and percent of multiple responses to each situation involving the use of electronic resources. There were 1178 responses and it was found that among all these responses, the highest percent (20%) was in regard to the situation of completing some writing. This is consistent with the above results.

Table 6.12   Situations using electronic resources

Situations	Frequency	Percent
To complete some writing	236	77.4%
To undertake a research project	212	69.5%
To gain new ideas	181	59.3%
To compare different views	158	51.8%
To undertake a new task	119	39.0%
To make a complex decision	103	33.8%
To undertake a routine task	92	30.2%
To make a simple decision	77	25.2%

Table 6.13   Situations using electronic resources (Multiple responses)

Situations of Using Electronic Resources	Count	Percent of Responses	Percent of Respondents
To complete some writing	236	20.0%	80.8%
To undertake a research project	212	18.0%	72.6%
To gain new insights/ideas	181	15.4%	62.0%
To compare different views	158	13.4%	54.1%
To undertake a new task	119	10.1%	40.8%
To make a complex decision	103	8.7%	35.3%
To undertake a routine task	92	7.8%	31.5%
To make a simple decision	77	6.5%	26.4%

6.5 Factors affecting the use of electronic resources

A five-point Likert scale ranging from 'strongly agree' to 'strongly disagree' was employed to mark the level to which respondents agreed with ten statements in order to identify the factors impacting the use of electronic resources. Table 6.14 shows the results.

Table 6.14   Factors affecting the use of electronic resources

Items	Strongly agree (1)	Agree (2)	Neutral (3)	Disagree (4)	Strongly Disagree (5)	No Response	Mean
Push of relevant electronic	35.1%	42.6%	14.8%	0.7%	2.0%	4.9%	1.33
Rarely find what I need	1.3%	6.9%	11.8%	48.5%	27.2%	4.3%	4.67
Information overload	5.6%	18.0%	17.4%	32.1%	22.0%	4.9%	3.67
Lack of supporting	5.2%	23.6%	17.4%	31.8%	17.0%	4.9%	3.67
Out-of-date Information	0%	11.5%	27.2%	42.3%	13.4%	5.6%	3.33
Time consuming	5.6%	16.7%	20.0%	40.3%	12.5%	4.9%	2.33
Inaccessible	4.9%	37.0%	21.3%	26.2%	5.9%	4.6%	2.00
Need for guidelines	4.3%	30.8%	29.5%	27.2%	3.3%	4.9%	2.67
Need for examples	8.9%	44.9%	24.6%	13.8%	3.0%	4.9%	2.00
Inadequacy of training/help	3.3%	14.1%	35.7%	36.4%	5.9%	4.6%	3.00

The relevance of electronic resources is an important factor affecting their use. 77.7% of respondents 'agreed' or 'strongly agreed' that relevant electronic resources should automatically be 'pushed' to end users based on user profile and interest. Among the other factors, those of training, help, examples and guidelines were all popular for improving users' skills using electronic resources. It seems that 'skills' and 'supporting equipment' did not significantly affect the use of electronic resources, given that web technology, search tools, and supporting equipment were common and easy to use. On the other hand, finding relevant, up-to-date, accessible information in a time-saving manner was something that appealed to most users.

This implies that ICT facilitates the use of electronic resources by making electronic resources more accessible, relevant and timely. This is confirmed by the fact that the introduction of a search interface across all online databases prior to the survey improved the effectiveness and efficiency of searching in the university surveyed.

The non-users indicated the reasons why they did not use the electronic resources. Among 12 non-users, five respondents were not sure how to use the electronic resources, while four of them were not aware of the existence of electronic resources, and the other three respondents thought that the resources were time consuming and inaccessible, and that there was no need to use them. Figure 6.5 shows the reasons and frequency for these non-users.

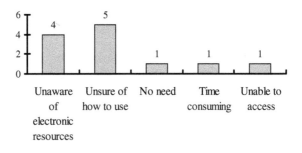

Figure 6.5   The reasons of not using electronic resources

6.6   Cross-tabulation analysis

The use of electronic resources is common in the university environment based on the descriptive results of the survey discussed above. The reasons for using them include accessibility, time savings, availability of wide variety of resources, availability of search tools, and the absence of physical space limitations. A majority of users found that electronic resources were useful to help them gain new ideas or insights, compare different views, undertake research projects and write theses or papers. They also integrated electronic resources into their work or study, and made their ideas available electronically. This leads support to the view that the conversion processes between information and knowledge occur during the use of electronic resources.

However, further analysis was needed to understand if there was any difference regarding the value dimension according to the 'user' and 'purpose' dimensions. Using five-point Likert scales ranging from 'not useful' to 'extremely useful', the value dimension was measured in terms of the usefulness of electronic resources. The purpose dimension was measured in terms of the purposes for accessing electronic resources, the situations where they were accessed, and their integration with work/study. The user dimension was measured by age, gender, position, seniority, education, use frequency, and access location. The chi-square test was employed to find out whether any two dimensions were significantly associated. The chi-square test calculates the probability that two variables are independent. A probability of 0.05 means that there is only a 5 per cent chance that the variables are independent of each other. Therefore, a probability of 0.05 or smaller means that it is at least 95 per cent certain that two variables are significantly associated (Saunders et al., 2000; Coakes, 2005). To ensure that frequency in every cell is not less than 5, some cells have been merged and chi-square test results have been recalculated.

Table C.1 in Appendix C shows the result of a cross-tabulation analysis between user's position and perceived usefulness. Excluding 12 non-users, the cross-tabulation analysis of the user's position group and the usefulness of electronic resources suggests that different groups of users value electronic resources significantly differently. Among the research population, a majority of academic staff (77.5%) and postgraduate research students (74.0%) believed that electronic resources were extremely useful. This might be due to their highly knowledge-intensive work and relative competence in dealing with electronic resources. Analysis also revealed that a relatively low percentage of undergraduate and TAFE students (37.4%) thought that electronic resources were extremely useful. The relationship between users' position and usefulness is significant, with a chi-square test result of $x^2(16) =38.549$ (p=.001). The result was reinforced by merging some cells, with a chi-square test result of $x^2(4) =33.021$ (p=.000) as shown in Table C.10 in Appendix C.

Table C.2 in Appendix C shows the cross-tabulation between users' seniority and perceived usefulness. The user group classified by years in their current position did not show significant difference in experience of using electronic resources. This implies that there is not a strong relationship between seniority and the use of electronic resources, with a chi-square test result of $x^2(16) =16.759$ (p=.401). Although all the users in the group of 'more than 25 years' thought electronic resources were extremely useful, the count is only 4. After combining this group with '5-10 years' and '11-25 years' groups, there was no significant difference between the '5 years and more than 5 years' group and the other two groups, with a chi-square test result of $x^2(8) =13.023$ (p=.111). The result was reinforced by merging some cells, with a chi-square test result of $x^2(2) =7.227$ (p=.027) as shown in Table C.11 in Appendix C. This might be because the cognitive capability of users does not closely relate to their seniority.

Table C.3 in Appendix C shows that users in different age groups responded to the perceived usefulness of electronic resources significantly differently. This was more evident after grouping users into 'under 30' and '30 and over 30'. 45.3% of the former group and 69.9% of the latter group thought that electronic resources were extremely useful, with a chi-square test result of x^2 (20)=20.049 (p=.000). The result was reinforced by merging some cells, with a chi-square test result of x^2 (2) =19.382 (p=.000) as shown in Table C.12 in Appendix C. This also conforms to the above finding given that most of the undergraduate and TAFE students were in the age group under 30.

Table C.4 in Appendix C shows that users with different education backgrounds also rated electronic resources significantly differently. Users with a PhD (75%) and a postgraduate (74.4%) qualification thought that electronic resources were extremely useful, while less than half of the rest of users thought so. The chi-square test result is x^2 (16)=40.584 (p=.001). The result was reinforced by merging some cells, with a chi-square test result of x^2 (4) =19.136 (p=.001) as shown in Table C.13 in Appendix C. This further confirms that users with higher cognitive capability and engaged in knowledge-intensive work recognized the importance and value of the electronic resources.

Table C.5 in Appendix C shows that the female and male users did not exhibit any significant difference in using electronic resources. The rating pattern for electronic resources for female and male users was almost the same, with a chi-square test result of x^2 (4) =150 (p=.997). The result was reinforced by merging some cells, with a chi-square test result of x^2 (2) =0.092 (p=.955) as shown in Table C.14 in Appendix C. It suggests that gender does not influence the use of electronic resources.

There was a significant difference between users who used electronic resources in their work or study and other users with respect to using electronic resources. Table C.6 and Table C.7 in Appendix C show the results, with chi-square test results of $x^2(12) = 36.295$ (p=.000) and $x^2(12) = 34.509$ (p=.001) respectively. The results were reinforced by merging some cells, with a chi-square test result of $x^2(2) = 19.110$ (p=.000) and $x^2(2) = 27.206$ (p=.000) respectively as shown in Table C.15 and Table C.16 in Appendix C. Furthermore, Table C.8 and Table C.9 in Appendix C show a significant difference between users who made their ideas or publications electronically available and those who did not, with chi-square test results of $x^2(12) = 25.031$ (p=.015) and $x^2(8) = 19.589$ (p=.012) respectively. The results were reinforced by merging some cells, with a chi-square test result of $x^2(2)$ =19.741 (p=.000) and $x2(1) = 11.524$ (p=.001) respectively as shown in Table C.17 and Table C.18 in Appendix C.

There is, however, no obvious pattern between the different purposes for using electronic resources in relation to their perceived usefulness. For users who intended to complete an assignment and obtain the answers to some specific questions, there was a significant difference compared with users who had not intended to do so with chi-square test results of $x^2(4) = 10.497$ (p=.033) and $x^2(4) = 20.161$ (p=.000) respectively. But for users who intended to gain general information, to gather information on a specific topic, to do a literature review, to write an essay, or to make a decision, there was no significant difference compared with users who did not intend to do so.

The conditions for the use of electronic resources appear to exhibit a stronger relation to the usefulness dimension. Compared with users who were not in the same situations, there was a significant difference in all these situations including comparing different views [$x^2(4) = 18.015$ (p=.001)], gaining new insight/ideas [$x^2(4) = 20.115$ (p=.000)], making a complex decision[$x^2(4) = 10.654$ (p=.031)], undertaking a new task [$x^2(4) = 17.697$ (p=.001)], doing a research project [$x^2(4) = 13.696$ (p=.008)] and undertaking a routine task [$x^2(4) = 20.852$ (p=.000)] except for those situations where a simple decision needed to be made and where writing tasks had to be completed.

On the other hand, multiple response analysis on purposes and situations in relation to the perceived usefulness of electronic resources, demonstrated a similar pattern no matter for what purpose and in which situation. This suggests that electronic resources are useful for a wide range of purposes and situations. When electronic resources are right for the specific purpose and situation, their usefulness is valued by the users.

In summary, there were differences regarding the value dimension according to the 'user' and 'purpose' dimensions during the use of electronic resources. The higher cognitive capacity users had and the more knowledge-intensive purposes where electronic resources were used for, the higher value electronic resources appeared. The relationship among three dimensions in the conversion processes between information and knowledge is shown in Figure 6.6.

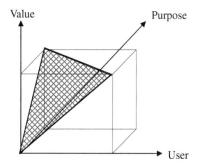

Figure 6.6   **The relationship among three dimensions in the conversion processes between information and knowledge**

6.7   Validity and reliability of the research findings

In order to ensure the validity and reliability of the survey results, careful attention was paid to the process of questionnaire constructing, survey piloting, survey delivering, data collection, and data analysis described as in Chapter 5.

Multiple indicators can be used to test the consistency of responses (Neuman, 1994). Phi (Φ) and Cramer's V, along with a contingency table and a chi-square test can be used to examine the association between two nominal variables (Cooper and Emory, 1995; Saunders et al., 2000; Bryman and Bell, 2003). A probability of 0.05 means that there is only a 5 per cent chance that the variables are independent of each other. Therefore, a probability of 0.05 or smaller means it is at least 95 per cent certain that the two variables are significantly associated (Saunders et al., 2000; Coakes, 2005). In Section 2 of the questionnaire, a question was designed to ask respondents the purpose of using electronic resource, while later in Section 3, respondents were asked about the situation where electronic resources were useful. The results show that significant associations exist between the purpose 'to make a decision' and the situation 'to make a simple decision' with Phi and Cramer's V=0.496 (p=0.000), x^2 (1, N=305)=75.090, p<.05, between the purpose 'to make a decision' and the situation 'to make a complex decision' with Phi and Cramer's V=0.479 (p=0.000), x^2 (1, N=305)=69.893, p<.05, between the purpose 'to complete an assignment' and the situation 'to complete an assignment/essay/thesis/paper' with Phi and Cramer's V=0.508 (p=0.000), x^2 (1, N=305)=78.761, p<.05, between the purpose 'to write an essay' and the situation 'to complete an assignment/essay/thesis/paper' with Phi and Cramer's V=0.415 (p=0.000), x^2 (1,N=305)=52.613, p<.05. This suggests that responses to similar questions in section 2 and section 3 are significantly associated to each other and indicates high consistency of responses in answering the questionnaire by respondents.

6.8 Reflections and implications

The survey results reveal that the overall attitude towards the use of electronic resources is quite positive. This is evident in the high proportion of users to non-users of electronic resources, the high use frequency, the high percentage of users rating electronic resources useful and the way that electronic resources are integrated into work and study. This positive attitude is further confirmed by additional comments from 84 respondents. Some respondents explicitly expressed their appreciation of electronic resources by saying that they were unparalleled, invaluable, essential, vital and extremely useful. One such statements exclaimed "*Best thing since sliced bread.*" Other respondents implicitly presented their opinions by stating that electronic resources should be highly promoted and that more electronic resources were needed.

As already indicated this positive attitude can be explained by the availability of wide variety of resources and their accessibility and time saving features, by the availability of search tools, and the absence of physical space limitations. ICT plays an important role in producing the positive results. ICT not only enables and facilitates easier, faster, and wider access to electronic resources, but also serves as the backbone of the electronic resources. ICT is of great benefit to users as is made clear by some respondents:

"I find using electronic resources a much better option by far in preference to a decade ago when you had to physically go to the library to search labouriously through heaps of information manually."

"Thanks a million for introducing the new gateway to electronic resources. It has made a once tedious task much easier and more effective."

"They save considerable amounts of time and give access to resources which may otherwise be more difficult to get hold of."

Despite this overall positive attitude, users also experienced some frustrations when they used the electronic resources. This frustration is usually experienced during (a) searching, navigating and finding the relevant source or information; (b) accessing it; and (c) downloading content. The causes of these frustrations are the confusing search interface, the amount of time spent on scanning and downloading, restricted access such as availability of computers, the Internet connection, and the requirement for login, password, and membership. These suggest that a more positive attitude towards electronic resources could be expected through the improved application of ICT employed in supporting the use of electronic resources. For example, a revamp of the interface for accessing electronic resources could render it be more user-friendly and direct users to find the information they need across diverse sources. A faster and more reliable Internet connection would increase the speed of download. This is further indication of the potential of ICT for improving the use of electronic resources.

While one respondent recognized that *"The potential for electronic resources is enormous, but currently I find the technology lacking. ",* other respondents pointed out potential areas where ICT could play an important role, for instance, *"collaboration among users with the similar interests", "document analysis tools", "promotion of communities especially those that foster networks such as blogs and those that enable the facilitation of shared information".* There were also potentials for opening up new modes of communication mediated through the use of electronic resources.

Another potential area for ICT is to facilitate the conversion of information and knowledge. The results of the survey show that a majority of users believed that electronic resources were useful to help them gain new ideas or insights, to compare different views, to undertake research projects and to write theses or papers. The results of the survey also showed that using electronic resources was part of users' work or study, and users made their ideas available electronically. Hence, the conversion processes between information and knowledge operates during the use of electronic resources. Furthermore, users expected ICT could facilitate the process, exemplified by the following attempt at searching:

"Interesting (electronic resources) but irrelevant to the current project topics can pop up in a search and if you are not careful you can go off on too many tangents. Initially I tried wide ranging searches of articles, downloading those of reasonable interest irrespective of relevance. To improve throughput I used Copernic Summarizer to identify themes. I used these as nodes in nVivo to automatically generate a summary etc. If necessary I used a scanner or PDF Converter to get Word documents. At the end of my trial throughput was great, but I did not fully appreciate the themes as I had not read the books/articles. Provided discussions stayed on my themes. I was OK but I was not comfortable that I had sufficient appreciation for a DBA. I have returned to a more traditional approach

being more careful in my searches reading and skimming books articles etc. and using nVivo to record my notes and comments."

The above attempt shows that ICT currently cannot do much in facilitating the conversion processes between information and knowledge. Artificial intelligence, intelligent agents, electronic resources and knowledge portals hold some potential, but human agents play the major role to analyze, understand, digest, absorb, synthesize, deduct, induct, and reflect on existing information and turn it into knowledge. Compared with converting knowledge into information, the number of users who are able to turn their knowledge into information is much lower in the survey. This involves the process of externalization, which is not fully supported by ICT. Although knowledge can partially be converted into artifacts, information and explicit knowledge, the tacit knowledge and the context pertaining to the knowledge are usually lost. There exists a wide gap between information and knowledge (Cecez-Kecmanovic, 2004). While the gap remains without ICT as a bridge, human agents need to actively interact with ICT to fill up the gap. In the mean time, there is clearly a need for the development of new supportive tools and technologies.

A better understanding of what facilitates the conversion between information and knowledge will help the development of such new tools and technologies. The survey sought to find out if there was any difference in using electronic resources along three dimensions. The 'value' dimension was measured in terms of the usefulness of the electronic resources. The 'purpose' dimension was measured in terms of the purposes of accessing electronic resources, the situations, and the integration with work/study. The 'user' dimension was measured using age, gender, position, seniority, education, use frequency, and access location.

The results suggest that different categories of users value electronic resources significantly differently. This was specifically shown in the different user's position groups, different educational backgrounds, different age groups, while the different user groups classified by years in current position or by gender did not show significant difference in the experience of using electronic resources. This might be because the users' cognitive capability did not closely relate to seniority or gender. On the other hand, user position and educational background were usually closely related to the nature of work/study and competency in the conversion process between information and knowledge. The age group showed the same pattern as the position and education group, since a user's age reflected and was consistent with his/her position or education in this context.

The survey showed that different users with different purposes were significantly different in terms of the process of using electronic resources. For example, there was a significant difference between users who used electronic resources as part of their work or study and other users. Furthermore, there was a significant difference between users who made their ideas or publications available electronically and those who did not.

The situations where electronic resources were used appear to be strongly related to the usefulness dimension. Compared with users who were not in the same situations, there was a significant difference in all these situations including comparing different views, gaining new insight/ideas, making a complex decision, undertaking a new task, doing a research project and undertaking a routine task, except for those situations where a simple decision had to be made and where writing tasks needed to be completed. This implies that the more complex the situation, the higher value the electronic resources appears to hold and vice versa.

Respondents used electronic resources for different purposes and in different situations. Multiple choices were allowed to facilitate responses to purposes and situations. The multiple response analysis on purposes and situations in relation to the usefulness of using electronic resources further confirms the strong association between usefulness, purpose and situation. This suggests that the electronic resources are useful for a wide range of purposes and situations. When the electronic resources are right for the specific purpose and situation, the usefulness is valued by the users.

However, there is no apparent pattern between the different purposes of using electronic resources in relation to their usefulness. For users who intended to complete an assignment and obtain answers to specific questions, there was a significant difference compared with users who did not intend to do so. But for users who intended to gain general information, to gather information on a specific topic, to do a literature review, to write an essay, or to make a decision, there was no significant difference compared with those who did not intend to do so.

While the dimensions need to be further explored and new tools need to be developed for the conversion between information and knowledge, the current technologies are not being fully exploited. The potential benefits of using electronic resources are not being fully realized (Adams and Bonk, 1995; Armstrong et al., 2001). This situation is well described in the following comments:

"I use what I know about and what I have time to find out about. I am sure there is a vast amount of relevant material that I don't know about. Not sure how to find out what that may be."

"So much out there and I could do with a great deal more in learning about them and how to make use of them"

"I often think the users have no idea about all the resources they could potentially be using. Apparently undergraduate students don't really take up this technology."

This suggests that factors that determine the effective use of electronic resources must be understood. The survey has conducted a preliminary investigation into the affecting factors. The results show that the relevance of electronic resources is an important factor, with 77.7% of the respondents 'agreeing' or 'strongly agreeing' that electronic resources should be 'pushed' to end users based on user profile and interest. This is consistent with the findings related to the user and purpose dimensions.

Finding relevant, up-to-date, accessible information in a time-saving manner is what satisfies users the most (Dawes and Sampson, 2003; Gandhi, 2004). One respondent's comment expresses the frustrations in using electronic resources as follows:

"To source a few relevant journal articles can take hours upon hours. It can get quite frustrating. You know the information is out there but sometimes it is so hard to find even when you are supposedly equipped with the knowledge of how to find it."

Among the other factors, training, help, examples and guidelines are all focused on improving users' skills using electronic resources. It seems that skills and supporting equipments do not significantly affect the use of electronic resources, given that web technology, search tools, and supporting equipments are common and easy to use.

In the comments made by respondents, there are other concerns about using electronic resources, concerns relating to awareness, taxonomy and classification, quality issues, copyright, training, and over reliance on electronic resources. These factors can be explored in future research.

In summary, the results of the survey reveal that the conversion processes between information and knowledge exist in situations involving the use of electronic resources. The results also suggest that different users with different purposes were significantly different in terms of the processes of using electronic resources; and that the relevance and the quality of information were important factors affecting the use of electronic resources.

One also can conclude that the use of ICT is essential to electronic resources. ICT plays an important role in using electronic resources. However, the potential benefits of current technologies are not being fully utilized and current tools need to be improved. New supportive tools and technologies need to be developed. Human agents need to actively interact with the supportive tools for the effective exploitation of electronic resources. This is perfectly described in this statement by a respondent:

"Can't live with them, can't live without them."

6.9   Concluding remarks

The questionnaire survey sought to explore the experience, perception and attitudes of the users of electronic resources and to identify the factors impacting on the use of electronic resources. It was used to illustrate the conversion process between information and knowledge. Conducted online in a university, the data about individual perceptions, expectations, experiences and behaviours in the use of electronic resources were collected and analyzed. The results of the survey test and validate the contention that the conversion processes between information and knowledge in the theoretical model exist in situations involving the use of electronic resources. It also found that different users with different purposes were significantly different in terms of the processes of using electronic resources; and that the relevance and the quality of information were important factors affecting the use of electronic resources.

Future research could extend the number of indicators for the dimensions and more factors could be investigated to better understand the conversion process between information and knowledge. The performance or outcome differentiating 'more effective' from 'less effective' conversion would be worth to be exploring with a view to making the most of electronic resources.

Chapter 7

Best Practices: An analysis of Business Cases

7.1   Introduction

Organizations have become increasingly aware of the importance of knowledge and knowledge management in recent decades (Nanaka, 1994; Spender, 1996; Martin, 2004). Tremendous efforts have been made to sustain competitive advantage through possessing and effectively utilizing organizational knowledge in innovative manners (Davenport et al., 1998; Rollo and Clarke, 2001; O'Dell et al., 2003; Beccerra-Fernandez et al., 2004; Hislop, 2005; Nissen, 2006). Knowledge management, as an effective means of improving organizational performance and maintaining competitive advantages, has been gaining increasing interest among practitioners in all types of organizations (Garavelli et al., 2002; Desouza, 2003a; Song et al. 2004).

Numerous knowledge management projects have been initiated and implemented in organizations. Lawton (2001) shows that eighty percent of the largest global corporations in the world have implemented knowledge management projects. Smalley-Bowen and Scannell (1999) find that one third of Fortune 1000 companies have included knowledge management initiatives in their strategic planning processes. An IDC report predicts that business spending on knowledge management could rise from $2.7 billion in 2002 to $4.8 billion in 2007 (Babcock, 2004). Those projects that report the achievement of excellent outcomes are often accepted as Best Practices in organizational knowledge management.

These reportedly successful projects have raised the level of interest in knowledge management (Smalley-Bowen and Scannell, 1999; Lawton, 2001;

Babcock, 2004). They have provided rich content and context for researchers and practitioners in knowledge management to further develop knowledge management theory and practice. An analysis of these success stories can help identify lessons and experiences learnt from the implementation of knowledge management projects. The type of knowledge objects incorporated in these projects can be identified. The ways that knowledge processes are supported in these projects can be recognized. The critical success factors for the implementation of knowledge management projects can be established. The insights drawn from these cases can serve as an important guide for those seeking to initiate and implement their own knowledge management projects (Rollo and Clarke, 2001; Davenport and Probst, 2002; O'Dell et al., 2003; Wolford and Kwiecien, 2003).

This chapter presents an analysis of business cases chosen from the Global Most Admired Knowledge Enterprises (MAKE) award winners, in order to further demonstrate the roles of ICT in organizational knowledge management and to identify the critical success factors for developing and implementing knowledge management projects in a changing environment. The chapter starts with a brief description of the Global MAKE award scheme. It summarizes the profile of MAKE winners. The chapter finishes with the conduct of a thematic analysis based on three major themes including (a) the knowledge objects incorporated in the projects; (b) the knowledge processes supported in the projects, and (c) the critical success factors for successfully implementing knowledge management projects in organizations.

7.2 Background to the Global MAKE award

Teleos and the KNOW network established the Most Admired Knowledge Enterprises (MAKE) research program in 1998. The MAKE program seeks to identify and recognize those organizations which create shareholder wealth (or in the case of public and non-profit organizations, increasing societal capital) by transforming new as well as existing enterprise knowledge into superior products, services, or solutions (Teleos, 2004). A Global MAKE and a Regional MAKE award are usually made to the winners annually in this regard.

The Global MAKE list is created based on the Delphi methodology (Liebowitz, 1999). A panel of Global Fortune 500 senior executives and internationally-recognized knowledge management and intellectual capital experts is employed to identify leading enterprises in creating organizational intellectual capital and wealth through the conversion of individual and enterprise knowledge into world-class products, services, or solutions. A consensus is developed among the panel's experts through several rounds of interactions and consultations (Teleos, 2004).

In the final round, the MAKE Finalists are ranked against each of the eight knowledge performance dimensions which form the MAKE framework. These eight knowledge performance dimensions are the visible drivers for intellectual capital creation (Teleos, 2004), described as follows:

- Creating an enterprise knowledge-driven culture.
- Developing knowledge workers through senior management leadership.
- Developing and delivering knowledge-based products, services, and solutions.
- Maximizing enterprise intellectual capital.
- Creating an environment for collaborative knowledge sharing.
- Creating a learning organization.
- Delivering value based on customer knowledge.
- Transforming enterprise knowledge into shareholder (societal) value.

From the group of finalists, twenty organizations are recognized as MAKE Winners based on the total composite scores. These organizations are actively engaged in knowledge management projects. They can be representative of best practices in knowledge management.

Forty eight organizations have been recognized as Global MAKE Winners since 1998. These organizations are from nineteen business sectors. They significantly outperform their competitors. Their total return to shareholders is nearly double that of the Fortune 500 company median (Teleos, 2006). The details of projects in twelve organizations have been published as case studies in websites, journals, magazines, conference proceedings and other sources. BULABS, Ernest & Young, and Microsoft are nine-time Global MAKE winners. BP, General Electric (GE), Hewlett-Packard (HP), IBM and Siemens are eight-time Global MAKE winners. McKinsey & Company and PricewaterhouseCoopers are six-time Global MAKE winners (Teleos, 2006).

7.3   Profiles of organizations for case studies

Twelve companies are large and internationally distributed organizations. Table 7.1 shows a brief profile of these organizations.

Table 7.1   A profile of organizations for case studies

(Annual sales are in billion US$ or Euro€ in 2004)

Enterprise	Years Founded	Head-Quarter	Country Distributed	Employee Number	Annual Sales	Industry
BP		UK	100+	103,000+	$285.1	Oil & gas
BULABS	1945	US	90+	1,400+	$0.429	Chemicals
Ernest & Young	1989		140	106,000	$16.9	Professional services
General Electric		US	100+	300,000+	$152.4	Electronics and electrical equipment
Hewlett-Packard		US	170	150,000	$79.9	Information technology
IBM		US		350,000+	$96.3	Information technology
McKinsey & Company	1926	US	40	11,500	$3.5	Consulting
Microsoft	1975	US	60+	57,000+	$36.8	Information technology
Pricewaterho useCoopers	1998		148+	130,000	$20.3	Professional services
Royal Dutch/Shell	1907	Netherlands/UK	140+	112,000	$268	Oil & gas
Siemens	1847	Germany	190	430,000	€75.2	Electronics and electrical equipment
Xerox	1906	US		55,200	$15.7	Information technology

Twelve organizations are distributed over some of the most knowledge-intensive sectors, such as consulting, IT, professional services, electronics and electrical equipment, chemicals, oil and gas. Table 7.2 shows the distribution of industry groups that these companies are in.

Table 7.2   The industry groups of the business cases

Industry	Enterprise
Chemicals	BULABS
Consulting	McKinsey & Company
Electronics and electrical equipment	Siemens, General electric
Information technology	Hewlett-Packard, IBM, Microsoft, Xerox
Oil & gas	BP, Shell
Professional services	Ernst & Young, PricewaterhouseCoopers

Many knowledge management projects have been implemented in these enterprises. Their experience in the process of implementing those knowledge management projects has been made available in the literature. Table 7.3 shows a summary of the knowledge management projects implemented in these enterprises.

Table 7.3   A summary of the implemented knowledge management projects

Enterprises	Knowledge Management Projects
BP	Multimedia Collaborative Network
BULABS	Customer Knowledge Bases
Ernst & Young	Network of Knowledge Centres
General Electric	Boundaryless Learning Culture
Hewlett-Packard	Learning Communities
IBM	Intellectual Capital Management (ICM)
McKinsey & Company	Client Knowledge Repository
Microsoft	Digital Nervous Systems
PricewaterhouseCoopers	Empowering Employees With Knowledge
Royal Dutch/Shell	Learning Centres
Siemens	Communities of Practice
Xerox	Integrating Knowledge

7.4   Thematic analysis

These twelve business cases have all employed ICT in their knowledge management projects. Table 7.4 shows how ICT was employed in the knowledge management projects in these twelve enterprises.

The twelve enterprises were early adopters of ICT in their efforts to support knowledge management. For example, HP's involvement in a company intranet is almost as old as the Internet itself. By the late 1980s, HP had used Internet technologies and tools, such as email, ftp, and usenet news groups for global electronic communications, for managing documents, for distributing software, and for training personnel (Information services advisory council, 1998).

Table 7.4   The application of ICT in the knowledge management projects

Enterprise	ICT Employed
BP	Intranet, video-conference, Internet, electronic yellow pages
BULABS	Online forum, knowledge bases, virtual conference rooms, virtual libraries and email
Ernst & Young	Database
General Electric	Intranet, video-conference, search engine, Internet
Hewlett-Packard	Internet, Intranet, Lotus Notes database, web
IBM	Lotus Notes Domino, the IBM intranet, email, linked telephone systems, community knowledge portal, content management
McKinsey & Company	Knowledge repository, database, Internet
Microsoft	Internet, database, intranet
Pricewaterhouse Coopers	Database, corporate intranet, distributed networks, search engine, virtual communities
Royal Dutch/Shell	Knowledge repository, database, groupware, intranet
Siemens	Intranet, websites, mailing lists, portal, databases, knowledge repository, data warehouse, collaboration tools
Xerox	Internet, intranet, multimedia, electronic whiteboards, PC-to-PC faxing, video-conferencing

The use of ICT benefits these enterprises in various ways. These benefits include (a) help an organization transform to a knowledge-based organization; (b) help share documents and best practices organization-wide; (c) help improve customer relationship management. For IBM, technology is not a solution in itself. It helps provide solutions that meet the requirements of its users for sharing, re-using, and managing intellectual capital in a networked team environment. ICT tools such as the ICM AssetWeb, the enterprise knowledge infrastructure, and its related solutions, Knowledge Cafe and Knowledge Cockpit have helped to transform IBM's business to one that is knowledge and asset based (Huang, 1998; Mack et al., 2001). Intranet sites at another global company, General Electronic, contain sophisticated search engines capable of accessing thousands of documents. Training modules are placed on the web, as well as best practices of various kinds in the organization. In addition, video-conferences are held frequently in which best practices are shared, and top executives communicate with employees in a timely manner (Bramhall, 1999). E-commerce and database technology provided the means for BULABS to collect large volumes of customer information, and to transfer accumulated expert knowledge to the point of customer interaction. This knowledge enabled BULABS to adapt to each customer relationship management (Buckman, 1997).

Clearly, the application of ICT plays an important role in knowledge management initiatives. Early in 1995, Microsoft initiated a project to investigate information sharing and to identify the appropriate platform for facilitating the sharing of information and knowledge. Until that time there had been little available as a central resource to house documents, findings, market research reports, and competitive intelligence information. The decision to use the Web enabled the organization to address the issue of sharing information and knowledge (Rosen, 1998). In BP AMOCO, the Internet made it possible to create a global procurement exchange by communicating information not just between one buyer and one seller, but between many individual participants simultaneously in real time (Choo, 1998a). The scope and geographical distribution of the Ernst & Young knowledge base and its users meant that technology had to be used as an enabler wherever possible. Lotus Notes was selected as the primary technological platform for capturing and disseminating internal information and knowledge (Baum, 1999).

The role of ICT in knowledge management, however, does not fully align to the integrative view of knowledge and knowledge management described in Chapter 3. In what follows, a further analysis is conducted to investigate the knowledge objects involved, the knowledge processes supported, and the critical success factors for successfully implementing knowledge management in order to better understand the role of ICT in the knowledge management projects implemented in these enterprises.

7.4.1 Knowledge objects

The conversion of knowledge objects involves the conversion of data to information, data to knowledge, information to data, information to knowledge, knowledge to data, knowledge to information, and conversion between different types of data, information and knowledge (Song et al, 2003). Knowledge management mainly deals with the conversion between data and knowledge, the conversion between information and knowledge, and the conversion between different types of knowledge, while ICT facilitates the conversion between data and information. However, the conversion between data and information is an integral part of knowledge flow. It is usually implicit in the conversion processes between data and knowledge and the conversion processes between information and knowledge (Nonaka, 1994). The seamless conversion of knowledge objects in the knowledge management cycle helps to generate new knowledge and leverage existing knowledge. An analysis of existing business cases shows that organizations have employed ICT to support the conversion of knowledge objects in their knowledge management projects.

Knowledge is converted to information by using ICT in knowledge management. For example, past experiences are leveraged at HP for technical support (Singh et al., 1999). During the mid-1990s, HP gathered the collective wisdom of technical support personnel into a sophisticated Lotus Notes database (Fryer, 1999). HP's intranet offered both the usual corporate information, as well as information and knowledge about the business units, products, functions and special interests. Customer support centres at HP had intranet access to problem-resolution information and to records of customer support requests and the answers given. The intranet also included a database of company-wide expertise created by HP employees. The content of the database was a set of expert profiles which described the background and expertise of individuals who were knowledgeable on particular topics. Employees could log into a web-based system, the Connex database, record their areas of expertise, and state their willingness to talk with anyone interested. In this way, Connex enabled HP employees to identify HP experts in important areas and provided pointers on how to contact them (Davenport, 1997a). Hence, HP's intranet has been described as a veritable goldmine of information (CIO Communications, 1999).

While knowledge is captured and converted to information by using ICT in knowledge management, information is also accessed and converted into knowledge by employees in organizations. In 1996, Xerox piloted Eureka, a system that electronically gathered and shared tips on service repair for technicians world-wide (CIO Communications, 1999). The company gradually established nearly five thousand tips, which were stored and managed in a web-based intranet system. Xerox technicians used the system at a rate of five thousand tips per month. They contributed one thousand new suggestions per month. In 1999, more than half of Xerox's 22,000 technicians world-wide accessed the Eureka system (CIO Communications, 1999). Information about customers was captured through both automated and face-to-face methods at Xerox. An information base, which contained the answers to 250,000 customer questions, was offered internally on Xerox's website. Employees at Xerox could search this knowledge base by product, technology, customer or customer type, to find out about customer use, to track the patterns of problems, and to identify the possible causes of the problem, ranging from maintenance to product design (CIO Communications, 1999).

Different types of knowledge have been converted, shared, and reused with the support of ICT in organizations. For IBM, intellectual capital consists of know-how, experiences, wisdom, ideas, objects, code, models, and technical architectures that are structured to enable the sharing of information and knowledge for re-use, to deliver value to customers and shareholders. The ICM AssetWeb provides organizational support centering on competencies, asset management support, and structured collaboration support. This tool, along with their ongoing work in the area of knowledge management, had helped IBM to serve customers better while making IBM a smarter and more nimble organization (Huang, 1998; Mack et al., 2001).

Knowledge is converted into information, which is, in turn, converted into new knowledge when employees access and reuse the captured and stored information. In this way, the dynamics of knowledge conversion processes is formed. When the two management consulting firms, McKinsey and Bain, merged, the merger led to the development of 'knowledge databases' containing experiences from every assignment, including the names of team members and a record of client reactions (Davenport and Prusak, 1998; Sveiby, 1999). Before the merger, Bain & Co. had created a 'client satisfaction knowledge repository'. Each client team was assigned a historian who recorded all facets of the project, including contract requirements, work assigned, the team associated with the tasks, client satisfaction and so on. The results were used to develop lessons learned, and areas for improvement, and to understand the needs of client and staff teams for future clients (Sveiby, 1999). After the merger, McKinsey's 'Knowledge Resource Directory' listed names against a well-defined set of expertise categories, such as familiarity with different industry sectors, technologies or business planning processes. The manager of each of McKinsey's practice areas approved these self-reported definitions. McKinsey executives found that the directory was helpful in understanding who had a general familiarity with a given topic (Dataquest, 1999).

Data can be directly converted into knowledge. This conversion process can be seen in the effort in seeking to obtain knowledge about e-consumer behavior. @McKinsey formed a strategic research alliance with Media Metrix in early 2000, giving @McKinsey clients exclusive access to a global database of click-stream data. Media Metrix, a pioneer in Internet and digital media measurement, had a panel of over 70,000 people under measurement world-wide, allowing it to track what online consumers do click by click, page by page, minute by minute. The audience measurement reports provided detailed information on the most-visited websites, how long users stayed per domain, the pages they visited, and demographic data on individual panelists. This information yielded eye-opening insights into e-consumer behavior. Those insights from McKinsey's clients were leveraged to build stronger e-business operations (Bjorhus, 2000).

Knowledge can be flowed among people, and between systems and people. When Price Waterhouse and Coopers Lybrand merged into a newly merged company, PricewaterhouseCoopers, in September 1997, a project called 'The Bridge' was implemented to make the important knowledge of both companies available to all employees (Drayton, 1999; PRNewswire, 2000). 'The Bridge' was a joint, integrated database that would identify the combined company's key people and their areas of discipline, and distribute some of the most critical content to the employees of the newly merged company. The objective was to blend the expertise of the two firms into a seamless, usable collection of knowledge and to make it available organization-wide (Drayton, 1999).

Knowledge was generated from the bottom up at PricewaterhouseCoopers. Knowledge managers throughout the world analyzed their users' needs, made recommendations and then aided the process of capturing the knowledge, reviewing it, and putting it into the system. Distributed networks handled the dissemination of collected intelligence. Employees could quickly search the firm's knowledge bases for information and contacts that they could use to serve clients more effectively and efficiently (Rothfinder, 1999). For PricewaterhouseCoopers, knowledge management was defined as "the art of transforming information and intellectual assets into enduring value for an organization's clients and its people". This emphasized that knowledge management concerns the conversion of information into something new, and that it should have lasting results (Drayton, 1999).

These MAKE winners cases demonstrate that data, information and knowledge all contribute to form knowledge objects in knowledge management. In addition, the conversion processes of knowledge objects were leveraged in the knowledge management projects. Knowledge was converted into information, and further into data with the support of ICT. Data was converted into knowledge by extracting the pattern from the vast amount of data. Information was converted into knowledge when employees accessed, reused the existing knowledge and generated new knowledge.

7.4.2 Knowledge processes

While these twelve enterprises made efforts to streamline the conversion of knowledge objects, it is noticeable that processes including those of knowledge generation, codification, dissemination and application were also the focus of their knowledge management projects (Davenport et al., 1998). It is these processes that help to convert knowledge objects from one form into another and facilitate the knowledge leveraging process within organizations.

Knowledge management projects in organizations attempt to support knowledge generation, although it is difficult to support the process with ICT. In 1993, Ernst & Young established the Ernst & Young Center for Business Knowledge (CBK). The CBK ensured that the firm's infrastructure and knowledge management processes delivered knowledge content which the firm's world-wide professionals could access and use anytime and anywhere. The CBK network consisted of strategic locations worldwide. "A key service provided by the CBK is the generation of timely proprietary research and analysis for Ernst & Young professionals"(Business editors, 2000). At Xerox, 'AmberWeb' provided electronic laboratories and conference rooms for group work, and less formal spaces where users could meet electronically and engage in the free-form conversations that bred many new ideas (Bauer, 1996).

ICT is able to support knowledge codification in organizations. An example of codifying knowledge was the compilation of a 400-page manual on alliance management at HP. The HP manual was converted into an online document and no longer existed in hardcopy form. This guide had become more of a 'live' document and was extremely user-friendly (Singh et al., 1999).

Many knowledge management projects aimed at facilitating knowledge dissemination. HP used the process of knowledge dissemination to route technical customer-support problems. When a customer reported a problem, the call or email message went to one of four HP hubs around the world. Operators typed the problem into a database and the file was directed to specialist teams in one of twenty seven centers. The database was shared by all centers and was 'alive', i.e., instantly updated so that every center had identical information about each problem at all times (Myers, 1999).

Xerox also created an internal tool to share information and knowledge in various communities across the company (Stephenson Strategies, 2000). To facilitate real-time collaboration and the exchange of knowledge in various forms, the system featured multimedia, electronic whiteboards, and PC-to-PC faxing (Bauer, 1996).

K'Netix is an interconnected system of knowledge bases used as a worldwide resource by BULABS. The network is used to share knowledge electronically; the information then being passed on to the customer. K'Netix puts the world's most knowledgeable experts at all levels at BULABS in touch with each other, encouraging group problem-solving and the sharing of new ideas and knowledge. The network encourages open, unrestricted communication among BULABS experts, and the free exchange of ideas (Buckman, 1997).

Knowledge management projects not only focus on knowledge objects and processes. They also focus on the integration of knowledge objects, processes and ICT. For example, one knowledge management initiative at HP was a mixture of knowledge and IT, with a view to identifying and codifying knowledge, and accelerating the transfer of best practices throughout a highly decentralized organization (Godbout, 1999). IBM Global Services has employed the ICM system to support intellectual capital and asset re-use for consulting engagement teams since 1994. This has involved taking practical steps to acquire, create, share, transfer, and use knowledge to develop and grow continually, and to anticipate and adapt to changing conditions. The project has established a solid foundation for knowledge sharing and re-use at IBM (Huang, 1998; Mack et al., 2001).

Although these knowledge management projects aimed to support as many knowledge processes as possible, knowledge codification and transfer appear to have been more fully supported than knowledge generation and application. This is probably attributable to the complex nature of knowledge and its dependence on human beings. In addition, the factors determining the success of knowledge management projects are diverse. These critical success factors will be examined in the following section.

7.4.3   Critical success factors

The knowledge management environment comprises many non-technological elements, which can be grouped as organizational and cultural elements. Organizational element involves organizational strategy, management, resource, and structure. Cultural element involves beliefs, norms, values, assumptions, and behavior. These elements can directly impact on the success of technology-driven knowledge management projects. Strategy alignment, senior management support, resource allocation, structure flexibility, people participation and knowledge management friendly culture in an enterprise are emerged as critical success factors in a review of these twelve cases.

Strategy alignment is to put knowledge management strategy in line with business strategy in an organization. It is important that knowledge management projects pay sufficient attention to the need to align business, technology, and knowledge management strategies (Holsapple and Jones, 2006; Jennex, 2006; Maier and Hadrich, 2006; Prat, 2006). For example, IBM placed knowledge management at the core of its business (Huang, 1998). General Electric's knowledge management efforts began with strategy and culture. Every employee at General Electric was indoctrinated with the core General Electric values within three months of their start date. Culture and strategy drove General Electric's knowledge sharing efforts (Bramhall, 1999).

Senior management support shows a strong management belief in the benefits of knowledge management. It is an essential prerequisite for the success of knowledge management projects (Jennex, 2006). This can ensure support from management that facilitates the implementation of knowledge management projects.

At General Electric, the idea of sharing 'best practices' among the different General Electric business units was fostered by management (Crowely, 1998). The directors of Microsoft's Product Groups understood the importance of knowledge management initiatives and worked with the Information Services Group from the start (Rosen, 1998). The CEO of BULABS was the prime moving force behind knowledge management at the company (Gordon et al., 1998).

To ensure the success of knowledge management projects, human and financial resources are needed to develop and maintain the necessary technology infrastructure. For example, Microsoft started with three dedicated people to build the intranet. By 1998, they have used about seven people to maintain it (Rosen, 1998).

Structure flexibility is another critical success factor (Jennex, 2006; Hendriks, 2006). At Xerox, there was no central authority or management with the introduction of 'DocuShare', an internal tool to provide electronic laboratories and conference rooms where users could meet electronically and engage in the free-form conversations across various communities. With no promotion or mandates, the use of 'DocuShare' blossomed in a grass-roots migration that started with a handful of researchers and embraced more than 25,000 employees from all corners of the company by 2000 (Holtshouse, 2000). At BULABS, a distinctive feature of their knowledge transfer efforts was the focus on direct communication between individuals, eschewing the traditional organizational hierarchy. As a result, the number of transmissions of knowledge between individuals was reduced to one, thus achieving the least distortion of knowledge (Gordon et al., 1998).

People participation is critical to the success of knowledge management projects since knowledge is created and applied by humans (Moffett et al., 2003; Maier and Hadrich, 2006; Prat, 2006). When Xerox established the Eureka system to gather and share tips on services repair for technicians, they discovered that the best incentive to get the service technicians to submit their tips was that of personal recognition. What worked for the system were the names of the validator going with the tip (CIO Communications, 1999). Likewise, At BULABS, employees were encouraged to access the Tech Forum, both to solve their own problems and to provide solutions to others' questions. Recognition schemes rated top level performers in the Tech Forum with respect to answering others' questions. These schemes helped boost employees' desire to participate in knowledge sharing (Gordon et al., 1998).

The knowledge management friendly culture is also a critical success factor. Culture refers to a set of values, beliefs, assumptions, and behaviors that are held collectively (Allee, 1997). It enables people interpret their experience in similar ways. Culture also influences the decisions that people make and how they behave in different situations (Rumizen, 2002). An appropriate culture is vital for the success of knowledge management projects (Moffett et al., 2003; Jennex, 2006; Kulkarni and Freeze, 2006). The establishment and nurturing of strong, committed, interlinked communities has enabled effective and efficient ICM system throughout IBM. Knowledge sharing had to be valued and practiced for the ICM system to work (Huang, 1998). There is also an emphasis on collaboration and cultural socialization at McKinsey (Sveiby, 1999). BULABS's management said that the culture change needed was the biggest challenge and believed that the company culture had to provide a conducive environment in which those tools were used (Gordon et al., 1998). Among the most important facets of culture is trust. Each employee must trust every other employee, because without trust in a person, one will never trust the information provided by that person. BULABS is said to have succeeded in creating an atmosphere where employees regard other employees as comrades moving towards a common goal, not as adversaries whose progress would impede their own (Gordon et al., 1998).

While some enterprises nurtured a knowledge management friendly culture, others adapted to the natural behaviors of employees and communities. AmberWeb at Xerox did not force people to adapt to what the technology required. It connected members of emergent communities and gave them tools that they might find useful. It also provided access to standard data and processes which helped connect people to the larger organization. The flexibility of the system allowed communities of practice to work in their own ways (Bauer, 1996). HP had seen interest in the value of knowledge informally arose among independent business units'. It was not a concept that was promulgated from the top (Davenport, 1996).

The factors mentioned above usually mix together and interact with knowledge processes dealing with knowledge objects. As such, they exert more impact on the technology employed in knowledge management initiatives. The knowledge management initiatives at HP were based on combining business processes with technology to create a collective corporate memory (Fryer, 1999). HP also used a personalization approach to support its business strategy, which was to develop innovative products. For that strategy to succeed, technical knowledge had to be transferred to product development teams in a timely way. The company channeled such knowledge through person-to-person exchanges. Remarkably, the company managed effective person-to-person knowledge sharing despite its size (Tierney et al., 1999).

At Xerox, AmberWeb was incorporated in the organizational infrastructure, not only among the researchers, but also among the corporation's product planners and marketers (Information Services Advisory Council, 1998). Xerox was "in the process of establishing knowledge sharing with all of our employees as a natural process of everyday work." (CIO Communications, 1999).

At IBM, ICM encompassed a system of policies, processes, personnel, values and technology and embedded it in the fabric of IBM's business operations. It enabled IBM's professionals to identify, store and efficiently re-use intellectual capital. The management framework addressed the elements which were critical for establishing a successful system of ICM and for initiating cultural and behavioral changes. It allowed the ICM team to create a foundation and culture of networked communities that helped practitioners to provide the best possible solutions to clients (Huang, 1998).

The Ernst & Young Center for Business Knowledge (CBK) ensure that the firm's infrastructure and knowledge management processes deliver knowledge content which the firm's world-wide professionals can access and use, anytime and anywhere (Business editors, 2000).

Knowledge objects are converted into data, information and different types of knowledge in the knowledge processes, while strategy, management, resource, structure, people and culture exert great influence during the interactions. The successful implementation of knowledge management projects depends on careful attention to all these factors. Figure 7.1 shows the critical success factors in the implementation of knowledge management projects identified in the business cases.

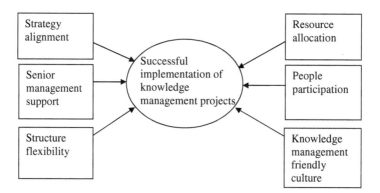

Figure 7.1   Critical success factors for implementation of
knowledge management projects

7.5   Concluding remarks

This Chapter has selected those business cases that reflect best practices in knowledge management from a variety of industries based on the list of Global MAKE award winners since 1998. It has conducted a deep analysis of those business cases in order to highlight pertinent issues that occur when undertaking knowledge management projects.

Although these knowledge management projects have been implemented using a variety of approaches, there are some common themes emerging from these cases. Firstly, these organizations were early adopters of ICT in their efforts to support knowledge management. A wide range of tools and technologies was employed in their knowledge management projects and played an important role in support of knowledge management. These organizations benefited from ICT in various aspects, including customer relationship management, internal and external communication, human resource management, business paradigm shift, and supply chain management.

Secondly, ICT supported the conversion processes between data, information and knowledge. Intranets and databases were used to gather and store the experience, expertise, wisdom, ideas, tips, suggestions from employees, record the history of projects. Knowledge bases or repositories helped identify the possible causes of the problem, track the patterns of problems, and offer possible solutions and answers. Apart from using ICT, knowledge managers and employees were actively involved in conversion processes of knowledge objects.

Thirdly, the knowledge management processes including knowledge generation, codification, transfer and re-use were supported by ICT in the projects as well. Moreover, knowledge objects, processes and ICT were integrated and interconnected together. However, it is noticeable that knowledge codification and transfer appeared to be more fully supported than knowledge generation and application, which were more dependent on human beings. There were not sufficient technologies and tools to facilitate these processes.

Finally, the analysis of those business cases reveals critical success factors for successfully implementing knowledge management projects through the application of ICT in organizations. These critical success factors include strategy alignment, resource allocation, structure flexibility, senior management support, people participation, and knowledge management friendly culture. The successful implementation of knowledge management projects depends on a careful attention to the above factors.

Chapter 8

Implementing a Knowledge Management

Project: A Case Study

8.1 Introduction

The relevance and importance of organizational knowledge for creating and maintaining competitive advantage drives modern organizations to use knowledge management as an effective means to facilitate the creation, organization, sharing, and utilization of organizational knowledge (Davenport, 1997; Wiig, 1997; Detienne and Jackson, 2001; Lehaney et al., 2004). This has resulted in a certain amount of success. For example, Lawton (2001) claims that eighty percent of the largest global corporations have implemented knowledge management projects with significant improvements in their performance targets. Smalley-Bowen and Scannell (1999) found that one third of Fortune 1000 companies included knowledge management initiatives in their strategic planning process resulting in direct improvement to their shareholder values.

There are, however, numerous evidences of experiencing less success with knowledge management projects in organizations. These include findings from a KPMG survey that many companies experienced difficulties in effectively using knowledge management technologies (KPMG, 2000). Such outcomes are likely to militate against the full utilization of the potential of knowledge management through the application of ICT in modern organizations.

In view of the adverse impact of unsuccessful projects on knowledge management, it is important to clarify the reasons behind the failure. Investigating the failure of knowledge management projects will not only reveal lessons learned for knowledge management practitioners and researchers, but will also reinforce the lessons of successful projects.

This chapter presents a case study of an unsuccessful attempt at implementation of a knowledge management project in a university environment. It first presents a review of knowledge portals and discusses the potential benefits of developing and using knowledge portals in organizations. It provides a brief introduction to the project, the background to and implementation process of a knowledge portal in a university environment. It analyzes the implementation process based on themes including knowledge objects, knowledge processes, and critical success factors as depicted earlier in the theoretical research framework. Finally, the chapter concludes with a summary of the main findings of the case study.

8.2   An overview of knowledge portals

Knowledge portals are web-based centers directing users to important and relevant information in organizations. They provide direct links to other sources of information via a single point of access to organizational databases (Gartner, 1998; Detlor, 2000; Dias, 2001; Malafsky, 2003; Benbya, 2004; Fernandes et al., 2004). Knowledge portals target a specific audience. They provide specific functions in a highly personalized manner including (a) content aggregation and delivery of information relevant to the audience; (b) collaboration and community services; and (c) application access for the target audience (Gartner, 1998).

Knowledge portals have the following characteristics (Gartner, 1998; Detlor, 2000; Dias, 2001; Malafsky, 2003):
- the simplicity of browser interfaces;
- the ability to gather information from disparate sources;
- intuitive classification and searching;
- collaborative information sharing;

- universal connectivity to information resources;
- intelligent routing, distributed services;
- flexible permission granting;
- external interfaces;
- security;
- easy deployment and maintenance;
- customization and personalization.

The main benefits of using knowledge portals include (a) easy access to the information distributed and scattered within an organization; (b) relevance to users with security access; (c) and access to valuable and strategic information hidden in heterogeneous sources (Detlor, 2000; Dias, 2001; Fernandes et al., 2004). Knowledge portals can be used as a means to promote the gathering, sharing and transfer of organizational knowledge (Detlor, 2000; Dias, 2001; Fernandes et al., 2004). Portals mainly offer index, taxonomy, publishing, search, personalization, integration and collaboration services for people with common interests, aiming at providing users with relevant and up-to-date information they need (Benbya, 2004). Examples of proprietary knowledge portals are Plumtree, K-station, Sharepoint portal server, Hummingbird EIP, Portal-in-a-box, XPS Portal, Verity K2, Knowledgecenter and so on (Malafsky, 2003).

Knowledge portals have gained considerable popularity among practitioners in organizations (Malafsky, 2003; Tsui, 2003). Fernandes et al. (2004) recognize that knowledge portals as a knowledge repository and transferring mechanism since ICT provide the best infrastructure to store, access and transfer knowledge in an organization. They demonstrate that the use of a knowledge portal achieved organizational objectives, such as reducing time, improving decision-making, increasing productivity and reliability. Baalen et al. (2005) show that a knowledge portal can facilitate the diffusion of knowledge among loosely coupled and often disconnected innovation projects.

A knowledge portal can impact on how people within projects share information and knowledge frequently operating as networks of practice. Portals are predicted to emerge as an expanding knowledge workspace that supports mobility, collaboration, and increasingly automated project workflow (Mack et al., 2001). Organizations are using portals as a key knowledge management technology (Detlor, 2000; Dias, 2001; Fernandes et al., 2004). However, technology alone does not guarantee the success of a knowledge management project. The following description of the process of implementing a knowledge portal in a university environment is a clear illustration of unsuccessful application of technology in support of knowledge management. The case highlights the point that an organization must pay sufficient attention to non-technological factors during the implementation of a technology based knowledge management project.

8.3   Project background

The case, in which a knowledge portal was pilot implemented, involved in a large, public, dual-sector university with strong international links. The university provides work-related education and training in eleven countries and has an established research profile. It offers over 500 education and training programs to more than 57,000 students, including approximately 6,500 full-time students studying overseas. Nearly half of the University's students are mature aged and many study part-time. Programs are offered in a variety of modes including TAFE certificates, diplomas and advanced diplomas; tailored training; bachelor degrees; graduate certificates and diplomas; masters degrees by research or course work; and professional or research doctorates. Students can undertake double degrees, dual awards and articulated programs that span TAFE and higher education (University Annual Report, 2005).

The university was structured into seven faculties at the time the case study was conducted. The faculty, from which this case was drawn, offered a range of education and training programs, from short courses and certificates through to diplomas, undergraduate programs and postgraduate programs. It comprised five teaching schools (School A, B, C, D, and E) and enrolled approximately 18,000 students.

To enhance the quality of programs offered by the university, an updated Program Quality Management System (PQMS) was introduced in January 2002. The PQMS provided an integrated approach to program documentation and included details and templates in relation to quality assurance processes in the university. The PQMS had been designed to assist program teams to access and store documentation. It accommodated the various records that program teams needed to keep, and provided supportive links and resources. It could be used either as a framework for developing a filing system for a new program, or as a location for indexing records which already existed. In either case, it should enable members of the team to locate the documents they need and to follow through initiatives and improvement activities effectively. The PQMS had also been designed to help program teams keep records for what they were doing in order to respond effectively to external audits (PQMS manual, 2002).

To put the PQMS to good use, School A decided to use a knowledge portal for filing either the location of program documentation or the actual documentation. The intention of the knowledge portal project was to enhance the dissemination and storage of information required by the PQMS, and to provide central access to all the relevant program information for quick and easy reference. The knowledge portal was pilot implemented not only in School A, but also over the other four schools in the Faculty.

8.4   The implementation of a knowledge portal

Documentation for the PQMS was stored in a shared drive at School A, supplemented with email attachments as a tool for document transfer and sharing. Although in itself a simple method which obviated the need for training, this nevertheless resulted in difficulties in identifying current versions of documents such as University and School based documents, processes and templates.

In response to these problems, a teaching and learning coordinator in School A initiated the knowledge portal project. A senior computer system officer seconded to the project, assessed a range of products and recommended a knowledge portal application, Microsoft Sharepoint Server 2003. This readily available software package and its capability for extensive customization for various user requirements resulted in provision of a user friendly, functional portal to facilitate the PQMS within the School. The senior computer system officer acted as the administrator of the server in order to maintain the content and security for users. A quality assurance officer loaded the portal with information stored in various locations throughout the School.

The knowledge portal shown in Figure 8.1 aimed to store and link the documentation for the PQMS, to keep information current, accurate and easily accessible to relevant users. The system automatically provided version management for the stored documentation. Access rights were determined by the administrator. Resources could then be accessed using keywords to operate a search engine or by navigating the directory structure.

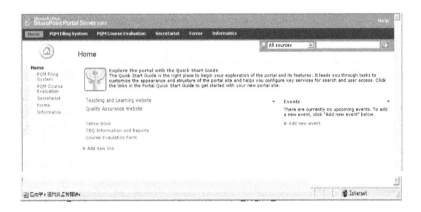

Figure 8. 1   A snapshot of the PQMS knowledge portal

The functionalities of the knowledge portal included (a) PQMS files (b) Course evaluation (c) Secretariat (d) Forms (e) Informatics (f) Relevant hyperlinks (g) School processes (h) Upcoming events (Manual, 2004). It accommodated the requirements from users at three levels: university, school and program.

After the knowledge portal was built, the pilot implementation occurred. An information session was held to demonstrate the features of the trial portal in March 2005. A number of users were invited to test the system. Interest was generated on a wide scale from other Schools within the Faculty and the University, with the knowledge portal subsequently demonstrated and trialed for use in other Schools. The project team aimed to implement the knowledge portal to such a degree that it could successfully be trialed on a broad level, and proven to be a sturdy, efficient, user friendly system with a widespread acceptance. A further test was planned for the second semester of 2005. Once the knowledge portal had been trialed for a reasonable period and by a sufficient test group, a decision was to be made on whether to proceed with the project or not. Although pilot users showed initial interest in the knowledge portal, active participation and continuous use did not eventuate during the pilot implementation. In September 2005, the quality assurance officer responsible for the content management of the knowledge portal left the School and subsequently the portal project was abandoned.

8.5   Thematic analysis

In spite of the fact that the project did not get beyond the pilot stage, there were aspects in this project that demonstrated the potential benefits of portals. Here are two typical comments from users:

"My personal belief is that the knowledge portal has quite good functionality and will show good usefulness for staff. The usefulness of the software is good and this becomes evident once a user has 'plugged in'. The knowledge portal allows for a broader spectrum of usage, as an example a user does not need to be on the University's premises to use the knowledge portal (this is web based software), this will make information more available. There is also no need for specialized software to be installed for end-users etc."

"I thought it was excellent. I thought it was an extremely accessible, well thought through method of collecting data."

Despite an overall positive attitude to the knowledge portal among pilot users, the system was not adopted by a single school. The main factors prohibiting adoption emerged as followed: (a) content; (b) strategy; (c) resources; (d) management; (e) process; (f) people; and (g) culture. These are now looked at in turn.

8.5.1 Content

The content of the knowledge portal was based on the documentary requirements of the PQMS which formed part of the quality assurance process. The major component was the electronic version of the PQM filing system handbook. This document was divided into ten sections including guidelines, management information, performance accountability, program information, program team, student and staff feedback, industry feedback, staff teaching matrix, improvement cycles and reports. There were other components ranging from the minutes of meetings, agendas, upcoming events, program structure, program maps, survey results, course evaluation results, and form templates to relevant links. Although ease of access and storage were said to be advantages of knowledge portals, the organization of the content appeared to have been one of the problems, as an interviewee observed:

"It didn't seem well organized. It didn't seem well-planned and well set up. My training is librarian. Librarian takes particular views about how information should be organized, and accessed, and found it again. I think it broke a lot of rules a librarian would not break. I thought the functionality counted upon good information management practice. The functionality did not complement what a library would do. It totally ignored."

Furthermore, the knowledge portal was lacking in some areas of content and was not relevant to the interest of certain users. Hence:

"The sort of information I need would never be put in the knowledge portal. There isn't a lot of information is going to put in that's going to be useful to me. I

couldn't see any point if I couldn't find any historical stuff. The thing I do a lot in my work is comparing things from year to year. It's most important to me. I might find out information four or five years ago. There wasn't going to be in there."

"It wasn't useful for my direct position within the School. If correct information pertained to my roles, yes, it would be very, very good."

8.5.2 Strategy

In addition to the content of the knowledge portal, the fundamental strategy and process supported by the knowledge portal were questioned. One of the program leaders pointed out that:

"There always is an ordered process, people at higher level will check on what is happening at lower level where the students and lecturers are. PQM system is for much higher level management. I don't think staff is really motivated. So staff wasn't interested in that. It's really hard to get staff start, to get motivated, to undertake it, to enter system like this. It's going to be difficult to ask them to document or record."

These comments could suggest that the PQMS imposed an extra workload on staff. It required considerable effort to make it operational. Often staff could not see any benefits for this effort. As a result, there was an obvious lack of motivation to put the effort into using the PQMS. This is further confirmed by another interviewee:

"I'm busy already. Why would I spend lots of time doing something if I don't get benefit? I can't find any benefit."

8.5.3 Resources

Although the objective of the knowledge portal was to reduce the amount of time and effort needed to maintain the PQMS, the resources needed for its management and maintenance tended to frustrate such outcomes. As one of the users observed about the extra time spent on the upload into the knowledge portal:

"I was also concerned that the Portal depended on staff spending a lot of time putting stuff in, and there is no one could do it. There is no one in the School whose job is to do this."

Supporting comment came from another interviewee who said:

"The most severe problem is lack of time to direct towards this project. This has been incredibly frustrating and has made the process to date difficult."

The system made additional demands on the time of the portal administrator, who collected information and loaded it into the portal. In this case, the portal administrator had other responsibilities in addition to managing the knowledge portal. There ought to have been a dedicated administrator to manage the knowledge portal.

"I think the responsibility should be full on one person, should be a dedicated person who manages that, because, then there is some integrity what actually goes on there, because we don't just want people to put what they feel it's important information right to the front, right there when it is not. Prioritizing what type of information goes there as well. We are going to use the valuable tool, which I believe we can do, just making sure the valuable tool has valuable information on that."

This is further confirmed by an interviewee whose position was at the university level with a statement saying:

"It does need a central administrator and I'm aware of difficulty in the current university environment."

The lack of adequate time and personnel clearly contributed to the demise of the portal project. The resources constrain the implementation of the knowledge portal in such a vital way that the process was influenced substantially by the availability of time and person dedicated to. School A, C and D stopped their pilot implementation because *"the person who was doing it has left."* School B expressed the reason as *"We did not proceed with our involvement due to staffing constraints in the School."*

8.5.4 Management

Senior management support is important for the implementation of IT projects (Fernandes et al., 2004; Jennex, 2006) and this portal project was no exception. Although the head of the School endorsed the project, there was no other evidence to show support from senior management. This was the case in other Schools as well.

"We've had five heads over the last four years. Lots of them have come and gone. That could be part of problem. I haven't noticed the head had pushed it at all."

"The head of School has not promoted it. ...The head of School doesn't use it obviously."

8.5.5 Process

It is clear from the literature that processes and practices need to evolve as implementation of these kinds of project proceeds, otherwise potential benefits can be diminished (Benbya et al., 2004; Fernandes et al., 2004). That this change process was absent in this case is evident in the following statement:

"The head of school notified staff information and attached it to an email. The head of school gets his personal assistant to stuff things up and she attaches to an email when she sends stuff up. It's attachment to email. We were told this is an important function document, and we should keep it in our email. The finance manager said that. She didn't say anything about the knowledge portal. This is a big file. They are closing up my email, right? It would actually be more convenient, probably to put something like in knowledge portal. No one used it. So there is no point moving in if no one is using it. If finance manager doesn't put things in there. If the head of school doesn't put things in. so you can't find things. Already all email

out and closing up our email. This is the practice for the school and university as well. The whole university doesn't. ......If you look at the website of faculty and you look at the services for staff, would you think it would be useful to provide a link to this thing? Here, I don't think so, not at all."

8.5.6 People

Equally important to all such projects is the full and early participation of users. This assists in the development of the systems and helps to ensure that it meets the needs of users. However, here is what one user had to say:

"I wasn't involved to set up. They designed and chose stuff and set it all up. ... We didn't think it was very good. That was a problem. I wasn't involved in setting up anything and in choosing anything. It should have done better."

8.5.7 Culture

Finally, the literature is clear on the fundamental importance of seeking some form of alignment between project planning and implementation and organizational culture. In this case the School staff was accustomed to working individually and sticking to their approach even though they expressed enthusiasm about trying something new and notwithstanding the benefits offered by introduction of the knowledge portal. This inherent mismatch between system and culture is reflected in comments from the staff:

"I have my own mechanism. More accurate than this sort of system..."

"I'm familiar with it. I've been doing it for years. So I didn't have to learn. I didn't have to remember the new password, extra password and log in things."

In summary, there is a wide acceptance in the literature that knowledge portals can provide an excellent infrastructure for accessing, storing and sharing knowledge. In this case, portal technology had the potential to enable users to easily access, store and share PQM information from various sources. Without the portal, keeping PQM documents current and accurate was a tedious task. Therefore, ICT in the form of the portal could have served as the backbone of this knowledge management initiative.

However, owing to a combination of the factors mentioned above, the system failed to gain acceptance beyond the pilot stage. In the circumstances the only likely source of positive outcomes from the project would be in the form of any lessons learned from the failure. Figure 8.2 shows lessons learned in the implementation of the knowledge portal.

One of the lessons learned is that a portal needs a well planned and organized ontology, taxonomy and classification, if ICT is to seamlessly integrate with information management in a knowledge management project.

Other lessons learned involve those to do with knowledge management processes and the knowledge management environment. Knowledge management processes need to be supported by ICT. If knowledge management processes are partly supported by ICT, then a mechanism must be devised to ensure that ICT seamlessly integrates with the needs and practices of human beings.

Moreover, insufficient attention to the organizational, managerial, and cultural elements of knowledge management environment impeded the successful implementation of the knowledge portal in this project.

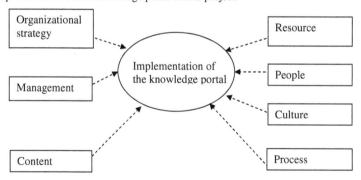

Figure 8.2   **Lessons learned in the implementation of the knowledge portal**

8.6 Concluding remarks

ICT offers an ideal solution for creating, storing and transferring information with added advantages of flexibility, customization and relevance (Fernandes et al., 2004). However, as this case has shown the technology itself does not guarantee the successful realization of its potential.

The failure of the adoption of the knowledge portal as a tool of knowledge access, storage and sharing highlights some of the factors prohibiting the process of implementing a knowledge management project. The lessons learned from this case demonstrate that knowledge objects, knowledge process and non-technological elements including strategy, process, structure, management, resource, people and culture are critical for the success of implementing a knowledge management project.

Chapter 9

A Novel Framework

for Effective Knowledge Management

9.1 Introduction

Knowledge has been increasingly recognized to be a primary source of organizations' competitiveness (Nonaka, 1991; Wiig, 1997; Lehaney et al., 2004). Knowledge management is a systematic process of managing knowledge assets, processes, and internal environment to facilitate the creation, organization, sharing, utilization, and measurement of knowledge to achieve strategic aims of an organization (Drucker, 1993; Wiig, 1997). Knowledge management is of strategic importance for an organization to gain and sustain its competitive advantage in today's rapidly changing environment. It is widely seen as an essential means for the survival and success of organizations.

Knowledge, however, is an elusive concept. The complex nature of knowledge offers many challenges to knowledge management practitioners in organizations, resulting in different approaches in practice (Nonaka and Takeuchi, 1995; Davenport and Prusak, 1998; Alavi and Leidner, 2001; Song et al. 2004). Among these, the technological approach is one that is commonly adopted in organizations. This approach focuses on the application of ICT in managing and utilizing knowledge in organizations (Ruggles, 1997; Song et al., 2005). For example, knowledge repositories are created to code and share best practices. Corporate knowledge maps are developed to direct people who need answers to those who have expertise (Becerra-Fernandez, 2004; Dalkir, 2005; Nissen, 2006).

The rapid advance of ICT offers unprecedented capacities and potentials for knowledge management. The enabling role of ICT in support of knowledge management initiatives is recognized among researchers and practitioners (Junnarkar and Brown, 1997; Hasan and Crawford, 2003). However, some researchers and practitioners would question the role of ICT in support of knowledge management owing to the failure of specific efforts at using ICT in support of knowledge management initiatives (Zack, 1998b; McDermott, 1999; Roberts, 2000; Stromquist and Samoff, 2000; Walsham, 2001; Butler, 2003; Desouza, 2003a; Desouza, 2003b).

This study has investigated the role of ICT in support of knowledge management and on how ICT can be effectively used for knowledge management. Based on a comprehensive literature review, a knowledge management framework was developed to investigate the role of ICT in support of knowledge management. The framework not only centers on the dynamics of knowledge objects and processes, but also focuses on the impact of the internal knowledge management environment, where organizational, managerial, structural, cultural and other related elements interact.

The research addressed the issues of (a) how ICT play an enabling and facilitating role during the conversion processes of knowledge objects within the life cycle of knowledge processes, and (b) how these roles might be affected by the knowledge management environment. The empirical findings were obtained from secondary data analysis, and the conduct of a questionnaire survey and a case study. The secondary data were gathered and analyzed to get a better understanding of current knowledge management Best Practices. In order to investigate the conversion processes of knowledge objects, the questionnaire survey was conducted to explore the experience, perceptions and opinions of respondents as regards the use of electronic resources at an individual level. To identify the factors that can determine success or failure in implementing knowledge management projects, a case study was undertaken to collect and analyze empirical evidence from the field.

This chapter presents a summarized discussion based on the empirical findings arising from the research. It presents a modified knowledge management framework in order to reflect the understandings and the insights gained from the empirical studies.

9.2 The roles of ICT in knowledge management

From an IT perspective, knowledge objects consist of data, information and knowledge (Davenport and Prusak, 2000; Tuomi, 2000; Alavi and Leidner, 2001; Song et al., 2003; Spiegler, 2003). Effective knowledge management processes move knowledge objects smoothly through knowledge generation, codification, and dissemination to application (Maier and Hadrich, 2006). They streamline the creating, capturing, classifying, organizing, transferring and reuse of knowledge. While knowledge codification and dissemination are increasingly supported by ICT applications such as knowledge repositories, the Internet, intranets and knowledge portals, the use of supportive technology for knowledge generation and application remains less extensive (Marwick, 2001; Gray and Tehrani, 2003; Malafsky, 2003; Maier, 2004).

ICT fully supports the conversion processes between data and information. Many successful cases of knowledge management as cited in Chapter 7 show that the data stored in database and data warehouse can be freely converted into the organized and meaningful information. Hypothesis 1.1, i.e., ICT can enable and facilitate conversion processes between data and information, is therefore supported. However, information must be carefully designed and well organized to cater for knowledge workers' needs in order to obviate information overload. ICT needs to be seamlessly integrated with information management to establish a knowledge platform for knowledge management (Malhotra, 1999; Detlor, 2000; Dias, 2001; Benbya et al., 2004).

New tools and technologies have been developed to enable and facilitate the conversion processes between data and knowledge (Fayyad et al., 1996; Merlyn and Valikangas, 1998; McDermott, 1999; Shaw et al., 2001; Garavelli et al., 2002;

Nemati et al., 2002; Zeleny, 2002; Liao, 2003). Data mining and knowledge discovery, for example, can extract patterns from the huge amounts of data collected and stored in organizational data warehouses. However, the prospect of turning knowledge into data is not so promising. A fundamental reason might be due to the complex nature of knowledge (Nonaka and Takeuchi, 1995; Davenport and Prusak, 1998; Alavi and Leidner, 2001; Song et al. 2004). The context attached to knowledge and the tacit aspects of knowledge are difficult and at times impossible to capture and store when the technological approaches are applied to convert knowledge into data. Hypothesis 1.2, i.e., ICT can enable and facilitate conversion processes between data and knowledge, is therefore partially supported.

Furthermore, tacit knowledge is often lost in the process of converting knowledge into information, albeit this loss is likely less than in the process of converting knowledge into data, where the separation of content and context, and the separation of data and metadata occur. It is disappointing that ICT can do little in facilitating the conversion processes between information and knowledge. Artificial intelligence, electronic resources and knowledge portals hold some potential (Nissen, 2006). Humans, however, play the key role in analyzing, understanding, digesting, absorbing, synthesizing, deducting, inducting, and reflecting on existing information and in turning it into knowledge (Offsey, 1997; Bhatt, 2001; Moffett et al., 2003). Hypothesis 1.3, i.e., ICT can enable and facilitate conversion processes between information and knowledge, is therefore partially supported. For the conversion processes between information and knowledge to be really effective, knowledge management requires new supportive tools and technologies (Fayyad et al., 1996; Merlyn and Valikangas, 1998; Marwick, 2001; Shaw et al., 2001; Garavelli et al., 2002; Nemati et al., 2002; Zeleny, 2002; Gray and Tehrani, 2003; Malafsky, 2003; Maier, 2004). Where there is little technology to enable and facilitate the conversion processes between information and knowledge, humans need to play major role and actively interact with ICT. In summary, Hypothesis 1, i.e., ICT can enable and facilitate the conversion of knowledge objects, is partially supported. The needs of knowledge management cannot be fully met by ICT, the contribution of which remains enabling and supportive in nature (Nissen, 2006).

ICT still plays an important role in knowledge management, despite its

---

limitations in supporting effective knowledge management. The majority of knowledge management projects use ICT as a backbone to achieve their knowledge management objectives, resulting therefore in success as well as failure (Tsui, 2005). Critical success factors are the minimum key factors that an organization must have or acquire to achieve its mission. They represent those areas that must be given special and continual attention to ensure success (Alazmi and Zairi, 2003). This study has explored the critical success factors impacting on the implementation of knowledge management projects, including organizational and social elements. The organizational element mainly involves the business strategy, senior management support, the organizational structure and business processes. The social element mainly involves the presence of social networks and the culture. These elements together help create an internal environment in which knowledge management projects can be implemented successfully. Without a knowledge friendly environment including critically an appropriate culture, knowledge management efforts are not likely to succeed. Based on the findings from Best Practice cases, Hypothesis 2.1, i.e., ICT must incorporate an organizational element for the effective implementation of knowledge management projects, and Hypothesis 2.2, i.e., ICT must incorporate a cultural element for the effective implementation of knowledge management projects, are supported. They are reinforced by the findings from the case conducted for this book in which unsuccessful implementation of a knowledge portal occurred. Hypothesis 2, i.e., ICT must incorporate non-technological elements for the effective implementation of knowledge management projects, is therefore fully supported.

9.3 A novel framework for effective knowledge management

The new insights arising from this study extend our understanding of knowledge, and of the relationship between ICT and knowledge management, and the relationship between knowledge management and the internal knowledge management environment. Knowledge is variously an object that can be manipulated and the process of knowing, and the assets and capabilities that organizations must align with their business strategies to gain competitive edge (Song et al., 2004). Knowledge management is essential if organizational knowledge is to be leveraged and sustained in a dynamic life cycle (Grant, 1991; Drucker, 1993; Davenport, 1997; Wiig, 1997; Detienne and Jackson, 2001; Lehaney et al., 2004). The role of ICT in knowledge management is to enable and facilitate knowledge management efforts.

Although rapid advances in ICT are likely to continue in the future, people remain the major players in the dynamic life cycle of knowledge, and ICT needs to support and integrate with people for effective knowledge management. The knowledge management strategy and processes must be aligned with business strategy and organizational processes (Holsapple and Jones, 2006; Jennex, 2006; Maier and Hadrich, 2006; Prat, 2006). Organization management, structure and culture must be 'knowledge-friendly' and help to build the capabilities an organization needs to achieve its strategy.

The extended understanding of knowledge, of the relationship between ICT and knowledge management, and of the relationship between knowledge management and the internal knowledge management environment emerging from this research lead to a further modification of the knowledge management framework described in Chapter 3. Figure 9.1 shows the modified knowledge management framework, which is made up of three tiers.

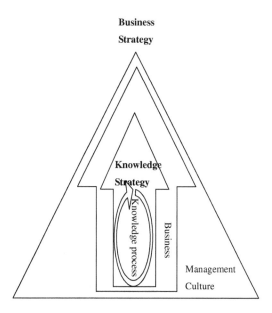

Figure 9.1   Three tiers of the knowledge management framework

The outermost tier illustrates the boundary of an organization, the internal environment of knowledge management and the major impacting elements. The middle tier is the business process. The objective of an organization is to establish its core business processes and coordinate managerial and cultural elements in order to achieve its business strategy. At the core tier, knowledge processes are embedded in business processes. Knowledge objects interact with knowledge processes. ICT is seamlessly integrated with people to convert knowledge objects and streamline knowledge processes, in order to accomplish the knowledge strategy, which must be in line with the business strategy. Figure 9.2 shows the core tier of the modified knowledge management framework.

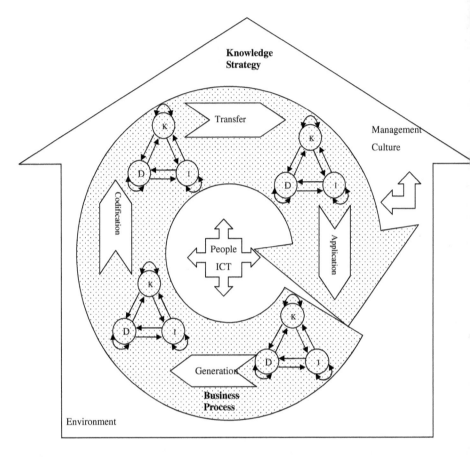

Figure 9.2   The core tier of the knowledge management framework

The innermost of the core tier is composed of knowledge object conversion processes and knowledge processes including knowledge generation, codification, transfer and application. In the processes of the knowledge life cycle, knowledge objects are constantly converted into each other and transformed into different states or forms within the same component, with or without the support of ICT. Figure 9.3 shows the interaction of conversion processes between knowledge objects and of knowledge processes with people and ICT.

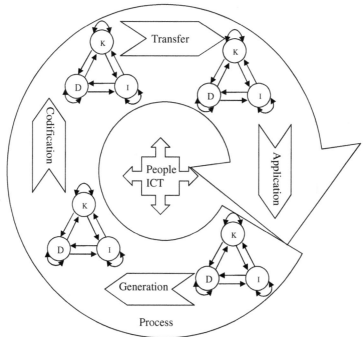

Figure 9.3   The interaction of conversion processes and knowledge processes

The conversion processes between data, information and knowledge bridge and integrate the conventional hierarchy and the reversed hierarchy in a cycle as outlined in Chapter 3. When new knowledge is abstracted from data and information, it can be explicated, captured and converted into new information and new data. This reflects the process of internalization and combination in SECI model (Nonaka and Takeuchi, 1995). When this knowledge is explicated, captured and converted into information and data, it can be the source of and basis from which new knowledge can be abstracted. This reflects the process of externalization and combination in SECI model (Nonaka and Takeuchi, 1995). The conversion within each component may be from one source to another, such as from people to system, or from one form or state to another by means of updating, aggregating, sorting, indexing, clustering, classifying, codifying, storing, retrieving, transferring, and communicating. In this way, the conversion process from any component in the cycle is continuous, iterative and evolving in a spiral fashion. The conversion processes between knowledge objects are closely related to the people who use them, and to the purposes, for which people use them. People are the major actors in the conversion processes and the knowledge management processes, with the support of ICT.

This framework can be used as a guide to direct knowledge management practitioners embarked in knowledge management initiatives. A knowledge management project must start from its grounding in the business strategy, business processes, organizational management, organizational structure, organizational culture, knowledge strategy, knowledge processes, knowledge objects, and people to ICT. The knowledge strategy must be aligned with business strategy. The knowledge processes must be embedded in business processes. The knowledge objects must be integrated with knowledge processes. The integrated and dynamic knowledge life cycle must be in harmony with the internal knowledge management environment, which is characterized by the nature of organizational management, and organizational structure and organizational culture.

The implementation of a knowledge management project starts from ICT, people, knowledge objects, knowledge processes, knowledge strategy, business processes, organizational management, organizational structure, and organizational culture to business strategy. This objective is to build the knowledge capabilities planned in the knowledge management initiatives and to ensure that the business strategy be reinforced through the implementation of knowledge management projects.

The knowledge management framework can also be used as a platform for assessing knowledge management projects. It identifies to critical success factors and the primary indicators for evaluating knowledge management projects. Additional secondary indicators can be introduced as the project unfolds.

9.4   Concluding remarks

This study has sought to investigate the role of ICT in support of knowledge management. By employing a hybrid research methodology combining a literature review, case study and a questionnaire survey, the results confirm that ICT plays an enabling role in knowledge management, but ICT enables and supports, to a relatively different extent, the conversion processes of knowledge objects and the life cycle of knowledge processes.

In confirming that ICT enables the conversion processes of knowledge objects, the research shows that this potential for conversion is limited to facilitation of the conversion of knowledge into data or information, and of information into knowledge. The knowledge life cycle is, therefore, only partially supported by ICT. In order to enhance such support, new tools and technologies are required to facilitate the conversion processes of information into knowledge, and of knowledge into data or information.

The research further confirms that while necessary for the successful implementation of knowledge management projects, ICT is not in itself sufficient to ensure such success. Although ICT can play an important role in support of knowledge management, the effective use of ICT requires that knowledge management practitioners pay attention to a wide range of managerial, structural and cultural elements. It is essential that key alignments are obtained between knowledge strategy and business strategy and that knowledge processes are embedded in business processes. Without due attention to these elements in organizations, it is unlikely that knowledge management will succeed.

Chapter 10

Conclusion

10.1 Introduction

Knowledge management has become increasingly important in the hyper-competitive environment in which organizations must increasingly operate (Drucker, 1993; Demarest, 1997; Wiig, 1997; Blumentritt and Johnston, 1999; Davenport and Prusak, 2000; Detienne and Jackson, 2001; Earl, 2001; Lehaney et al., 2004; Cepeda, 2006). Practitioners have been making tremendous efforts to apply the principles and techniques of knowledge management, while researchers have endeavored to better understand them.

This study has attempted to advance the understanding of knowledge and knowledge management, and in particular the relationship between ICT and knowledge management, and between knowledge management and the internal knowledge management environment. The investigation began with identification of the research problem and a statement of the research question and hypotheses, and the selection of a research methodology. It then proceeded to its implementation in the form of a survey and a case study, and the analysis of empirical studies including a survey, a case study and secondary case data, leading to the development of a novel framework for knowledge management.

This chapter summarizes the findings and implications of this study. It discusses the limitations of the study, together with some suggestions for future research directions in this area.

10.2 Main conclusions drawn from research findings

As knowledge has become a key to gaining and sustaining competitive advantage, organizations have been striving to reap the value of intellectual assets through knowledge management. ICT has been widely employed in knowledge management projects with evidence for both positive and negative outcomes. An investigation into the theory and practice of knowledge management suggests that there is a lack of a clear understanding of the relationship between ICT and knowledge management. Such a missing link in the literature may have impeded realization of the potential of ICT in organizational knowledge management practices. This has made it difficult for knowledge management researchers and practitioners to understand the impact of ICT on knowledge management and to make full use of ICT potential in the field of knowledge management. As a result, there is a need to investigate the role of ICT in knowledge management, and to identify those factors prohibiting and facilitating the realization of ICT potential in knowledge management in order to achieve effective use of ICT in enabling and supporting knowledge management.

This study has sought to shed further light on the nature of the relationship between ICT and knowledge management. The central research questions were "what role can ICT play in knowledge management?" and "how ICT can be used effectively in knowledge management?" More specifically, this research included two sets of subsidiary questions from the perspectives of (a) knowledge objects and processes, and (b) knowledge management projects.

In investigating the relationship between ICT and knowledge management, two sets of hypotheses were proposed: (a) whether ICT enables and facilitates the conversion processes between knowledge objects, and (b) whether the internal environment for knowledge management impacts the effective implementation of a knowledge management project. To test the hypotheses, a combination of qualitative and quantitative research methodologies including theoretical induction, continuous literature review, secondary data analysis, and the conduct of an online questionnaire survey and a case study was adopted in this study. A research framework was established based on the literature review and theoretical induction. A questionnaire survey and a case study were conducted to obtain empirical data and to test and validate research hypotheses. To get a better understanding of current knowledge management best practices, secondary data were gathered and analyzed. In order to investigate the conversion processes of knowledge objects, an online survey was used to explore the experience, perceptions and opinions of respondents on the use of electronic resources at an individual level. To identify the factors that can determine success or failure in implementing knowledge management projects, a case study involving the pilot implementation of a knowledge portal was undertaken to collect and analyze empirical evidence from the field.

The results of the study partially support the hypotheses proposed. They provide a qualified support for the use of ICT in knowledge management. On the one hand, ICT is confined to playing an important role in support of knowledge management. Indeed this role is so pervasive that it is almost impossible to initiate and implement a knowledge management project without ICT. The role of ICT as an enabler in knowledge management opens opportunity for ICT contributes to the area of knowledge management and makes ICT support knowledge generation, codification, dissemination and application possible. This enabling role is clearly established and is shown both in the conversion processes between knowledge objects and in wider knowledge management processes. On the other hand, the role of ICT as a facilitator realizes the potential of ICT in support of knowledge management and effectuates the objectives of knowledge management projects. This facilitating role is still limited and is not as evident as it is as an enabler.

In the conversion processes between information and knowledge, humans play the major role. Although ICT can potentially enhance the process of converting existing information into knowledge, in reality it is people that are needed to analyze, digest, absorb, and synthesize the information available and to apply it to particular tasks (McDermott, 1999; Stromquist and Samoff, 2000; Roberts, 2000; Walsham, 2001; Butler, 2003; Desouza, 2003a; Desouza, 2003b; Zack, 1998b). Likewise, the process of turning new knowledge into information cannot be effected solely by ICT. While new knowledge can on occasion be converted into information and embedded in artifacts and processes, tacit knowledge and the context pertaining to the new knowledge are much more difficult to capture and convey.

In addition, there continue to be limits to the extent to which ICT can facilitate and support the operation of knowledge processes. Hence, whereas ICT can enable and facilitate knowledge codification and dissemination, it is much less effective when it comes to the matter of knowledge creation.

Furthermore, the role that ICT plays in knowledge management is secondary to that played by a range of organizational and social factors. Drawing on evidence from both successful and unsuccessful implementations of ICT in knowledge management, and on empirical evidence from this research, the role and limitations of ICT in knowledge management are further clarified. The factors impacting the effective use of ICT in knowledge management include business strategy, business processes, resources, management, structure, culture and people. ICT must be incorporated with people, in line with knowledge management strategy and processes to develop knowledge capabilities, which must be embedded in business processes and aligned with business strategy in a knowledge friendly environment. Without due attention to these aspects, the contribution of ICT to the success of knowledge management projects will inevitably be limited and ultimately will be inconclusive.

10.3 The main contributions of the research

This study provides two sets of contributions to the existing body of knowledge in knowledge management. The first set is conceptual in nature, leading to the development of theory. The second set is practical in nature, resulting in guidelines for practitioners in the field of knowledge management.

This study contributes to the theoretical domain of knowledge management in the following ways: (a) it provides a broader perspective on the ways in which knowledge objects can be integrated with knowledge processes; (b) it reinforces understanding of the extended conversion model of data, information and knowledge;

(c) it investigates three dimensions relating to the conversion processes between information and knowledge, and puts abstract notions into a specific setting; (d) it identifies critical success factors for implementing a knowledge management project; (e) it presents a novel knowledge management framework integrating knowledge objects, knowledge processes with the internal knowledge management environment; (f) it clarifies ICT's role in support of knowledge management as both an enabler and facilitator; (g) it identifies the areas where technologies are available and/or needed to support knowledge management.

The broader view taken of knowledge in this research, synthesizes different views of knowledge as object, process, resource and capacity. Knowledge management processes are closely intertwined into knowledge objects, forming a dynamic life cycle of knowledge. This knowledge life cycle becomes the focus of organizational knowledge management and constitutes the core of knowledge management efforts. The cycle interacts with organizational environmental elements such as organizational strategy, resources, management, structure, culture, people and technology infrastructure, while knowledge resources are deployed and knowledge capacity is built.

The knowledge object conversion model synthesizes the conventional hierarchy and the reversed hierarchy of knowledge object conversion. It facilitates a better understanding of the relationships between data, information and knowledge, depicting a holistic, dynamic and evolving cycle among the three constructs of data, information and knowledge.

Three dimensions, user, purpose and value, provide a measure for the conversion processes between information and knowledge. When the information is right both for the purpose and the user, the value is regarded as high, and consequently, converted into knowledge for the user and purpose in question. On the contrary, when the information is not right for either user or purpose, its value is not regarded as high and consequently, remains as information for the user and purpose in question.

The critical success factors for implementing a knowledge management project using ICT include strategy, resource, structure, management, people, and culture. They constitute the internal knowledge management environment, prohibiting and facilitating the effective utilization of ICT in knowledge management. The successful implementation of knowledge management projects requires careful attention to the above factors.

ICT's role in knowledge management is examined as both an enabler and facilitator in terms of: (a) support of the conversion processes of knowledge objects; and (b) support of knowledge processes. The areas where ICT is available and/or needed to support the knowledge object conversion processes and knowledge processes are therefore identified.

Based on the above understanding of knowledge, of the relationship between ICT and knowledge management, and of the relationship between knowledge management and the internal knowledge management environment, a novel knowledge management framework has been developed. It is composed of three tiers, including knowledge management process, business process and the internal knowledge management environment. This framework emphasizes the holistic integration of the conversion processes of knowledge objects, of knowledge processes, business processes and the internal knowledge management environment. It also emphasizes the complementarity that must exist between ICT and people in order to achieve the objectives of an organizational knowledge management strategy.

In addition to the theoretical contributions, this study will also have practical implications. Firstly, the knowledge management framework can serve as a base from which an organization launches its knowledge management initiative. Practitioners can plan their knowledge management projects with the guidelines provided by the framework. They can start by aligning the proposed knowledge management strategy with their business strategy. Following introduction of the knowledge management strategy, the knowledge processes can be embedded in their business processes. A combination of people and technology will be employed to leverage these knowledge processes.

The implementation can proceed in the opposite direction to make sure that knowledge management project helps to accomplish the business strategy. The implementation of a knowledge management project starts from ICT, people, knowledge objects, knowledge processes, knowledge strategy, business processes, organizational management, organizational structure, and organizational culture to business strategy. The objective is to build the knowledge capabilities planned in the knowledge management initiatives and to ensure that the business strategy be reinforced through the implementation of knowledge management projects. The framework could provide practitioners in the field of knowledge management with a roadmap in planning and implementing ICT for knowledge management.

Secondly, this study in presenting a broader view of knowledge and knowledge management to practitioners could reinforce the message that a careful attention should be paid to the conversion processes of knowledge objects and knowledge processes by focusing on people, with support of ICT.

Thirdly, this study could help inform practitioners about the critical success factors for the implementation of knowledge management projects and of the need to seamlessly integrate related elements in order to effectively utilize ICT for knowledge management. Finally it could be used to help develop an evaluation mechanism to assess the outcomes of knowledge management projects employing ICT.

10.4 The limitations of the research

Although this study contributes to the body of research and practice in the field of knowledge management and in the role of ICT in knowledge management, it has several limitations described in what follows.

The first limitation is that the scope of the investigation of knowledge objects focused solely on individuals and excluded any assessment at collective levels such as those of teams, functional groups, organizations and the inter-organizational level. The conversion processes of knowledge objects at the collective level may not be the same as at the individual level. There is therefore considerable scope for future research into the dimensions and conversion processes between knowledge objects at the collective level.

The second limitation is that only aspects of the internal knowledge management environment were studied. External environment factors such as customers, suppliers, and competitors have not been explored in this research due to time and resource constraints. The factors impacting on organizational knowledge management can be extended to address issues of the external environment in future research.

The third limitation is that coverage of cases of successful knowledge management organizations was restricted to those for which case reports were accessible in the public domain. Proprietary cases available for a fee have been excluded. Most of the accessible and published cases appeared to be studies of large and internationally distributed organizations. Cases of small and medium sized organizations were relatively less common in published form and were difficult to access. These organizations might have a different strategy and approach to knowledge management and different critical success factors, and hence future research might be addressed to the circumstances of these smaller and medium sized organizations.

The fourth limitation involves the scope of empirical investigations, which is the circumstance of a higher education organization. The results must therefore be validated against other types of organizations. Moreover, the questionnaire survey was a cross-sectional study, which provided a snapshot at a certain point in time. A longitudinal study would be required to obtain further insights into the role of ICT in support of knowledge management over extended time periods. In addition, the 'lessons learned' element only involved the pilot implementation of a knowledge portal. A full implementation of a knowledge management project could be required to reveal more lessons learned as well as details about critical success factors.

The fifth limitation of this study is that it was conducted in Australia. Although knowledge management projects implemented in other regions have been collected and analyzed for this study, the primary data were collected in Australia. Other regions with different cultures may show different results.

These limitations may affect the interpretation and generalization of the results. The findings need to be interpreted and applied with care.

10.5 Future research

Despite increasing interest in knowledge management research and practice in recent decades, knowledge management is still a relatively new area which lacks generally accepted frameworks, models and theories (Earl, 2001). This study was explorative in that it sought to develop a framework to depict the relationships between knowledge and knowledge management, the relationships between ICT and knowledge management, and the relationships between knowledge management and the internal knowledge management environment. Although this framework contributes to the existing research arena of knowledge management, it should preferably be used as a research foundation to trigger further investigation into the relationship between knowledge, knowledge management and ICT. Potential areas for future research include:

- Application of the framework to different projects, different organizations, and different regions for further validation and generalization.
- Additional dimensions need to be considered in investigating the conversion processes between information and knowledge.
- Additional measurable variables for the evaluations of projects, including external environment variables can be extended to explore the factors impacting on organizational knowledge management.
- Additional research into improved integration between ICT and human agents.

10.6 Concluding remarks

This study sought to investigate the role of ICT in knowledge management and the factors impacting the effective use of ICT in knowledge management. Its findings could provide practitioners in the field of knowledge management with a framework for planning and implementing ICT within knowledge management. Using this framework, practitioners could pay due attention to critical success factors and hence effectively utilize ICT for knowledge management. The results of this study also enable a better understanding of the relationship of ICT and knowledge management.

As knowledge management and ICT evolve and advance, ICT will play more important roles in support of knowledge management, moving towards the point where ICT could become embedded and inseparable in the conversion processes of knowledge objects and knowledge processes. This could enhance the contribution of knowledge management as an integral part of business process and strategy, in harmony with all aspects of organizational, structural, cultural and social elements.

References

Ackerman M.S. (2000). The intellectual challenge of CSCW: the gap between social requirements and technical feasibility. *Human-computer Interaction* **15**: 179-203.

Adams J.A. and Bonk S.C. (1995). Electronic information technologies and resources: use by university faculty and faculty preferences for related library services. *College and Research Libraries* **56**: 119-131.

Al-Ali N. (2002). *Comprehensive Intellectual Capital Management: Step-By-Step*. John Wiley & Sons: New York, NY.

Alavi M. (1999). Managing organisational knowledge. In: Zmud R. (Ed.) *Framing the Domains of IT Management: Projecting the future through the past*. Pinnaflex Educational Resources, Inc. 15-28.

Alavi M. and Leidner D.E. (1999). Knowledge management systems: emerging views and practices from the field. In: *Proceedings of the 32nd Annual Hawaii International Conference on System Sciences*.

Alazmi M. and Zairi M. (2003). Knowledge management critical success factors. *Total Quality Management* **14**(2):199-204

Alavi M. and Leidner D.E. (2001). Knowledge management and knowledge management systems: Conceptual foundations and research issues. *MIS Quarterly* **25**(1): 107-136.

Allee V. (1997) *The knowledge evolution: expanding organizational intelligence.* Butterworth-Heinemann, Burlington, MA

Allee V. (2003) *The future of knowledge: increasing prosperity through value networks.* Butterworth-Heinemann, Burlington, MA

Anderson J.R. (1983). *The Architecture of Cognition.* Harvard University Press: Cambridge, MA.

Angus J., Patel J. and Harty J. (1998). Knowledge management cosmology. *Information Week,* March.

Argyris C. and Schon D. (1978). *Organizational Learning: a Theory of Action Perspective.* Addison Wesley: Reading, MA

Armstrong C., Fenton R., Lonsdale R., Stoker D., Thomas R. and Urquhart C. (2001). A study of the use of electronic information systems by higher education students in the UK. *Program* **35**(3): 241–262.

Arthur Andersen and APQC (1996). The knowledge management assessment tool: external benchmarking version. Winter.

Assudani R. (2005). Catching the chameleon: understanding the elusive term *knowledge.* *Journal of Knowledge Management,* **9**(2): 31–44.

Baalen van P., Bloemhof J. and Heck van E. (2005). Knowledge sharing in an emerging network of practice. *European Management Journal,* June **23**(3): 300–314.

Babcock P. (2004). Shedding light on knowledge management. *HR Magazine* **49**(5): 46-50.

Bacon F. (1597). *Religious Meditations, of Heresies.*

Bansler J.P. and Havn E. (2004). Exploring the role of network effects in IT implementation: the case of knowledge repositories. *Information Technology & People* **17**(3): 268-285.

Barney J.B. (1991). Firm resources and sustained competitive advantage. *Journal of Management* **17**:99-120.

Bauer B. (1996). The Xerox web: matters of connection.
www.businessinnovation.ey.com/mko/grdwk.html

Baum B. (1999). The knowledge advantage: selling knowledge on the net: the 'Ernie story'.
www.businessinnovation.ey.com/research/knowle/KA5/sellknow.htm

Becerra-Fernandez I., Gonzalez A. and Sabherwal R. (2004). Knowledge management: challenges, solutions, and technologies. Pearson Prentice Hall, New Jersey.

Becerra-Fernandez I. and Sabherwal R. (2006). ICT and knowledge management systems. In: Schwartz D.G (Ed.), *Encyclopedia of Knowledge Management.* Idea Group Reference: Hershey, PA: 230-236

Beckman T.J. (1997). A methodology for knowledge management. In: *Proceedings of the IASTED International Conference on AI and Soft Computing.*

Beckman T.J. (1999). The current state of knowledge management. In: Liebowittz J. (Ed.), *Knowledge Management Handbook.* CRC Press: London

Benbya H., Passiante G. and Belbaly N.A. (2004). Corporate portal: a tool for knowledge management synchronization. *International Journal of Information Management* **24**: 201-220.

Berdrow I. and Lane H.W. (2003). International joint ventures: creating value through successful knowledge management. *Journal of World Business* **38**(1): 15-30.

Bergeron B. (2003). *Essentials of Knowledge Management.* John Wiley &Sons: Hoboken, New Jersey.

Bhatt G. (2001). Knowledge management in organizations: examining the interaction between technologies, techniques and people. *Journal of Knowledge Management* **5**(1): 68-75.

Bhatt G. (2002). Management strategies for individual and organizational knowledge. *Journal of Knowledge Management* **6**(1): 31-39.

Binney D. (2001). The KM spectrum: understanding the KM landscape. *Journal of Knowledge Management* **5**(1): 33-42.

Bjorhus J. (2000). Mckinsey joins E-commerce fray. *www.mercurycenter.com/svtech/news/indepth/docs/mckins060800.htm*

Blacker F. (1995). Knowledge, knowledge workers and organizations: an overview and interpretation. *Organization Studies* **16**(6): 1021-1046.

Blacker F., Reed M. and Whitaker A. (1993). Knowledge workers and contemporary organization. *Journal of Management Studies* **30**(6): 851-862.

Blumentritt R. and Johnston R. (1999). Towards a strategy for management. *Technology Analysis & Strategy Management* **11**(3): 287-300.

Bohn R. (1994). Measuring and managing technological knowledge. *Sloan Management Review* **Fall**: 61-73.

Boist M.H. (1998). *Knowledge Assets: Securing Competitive Advantage in the Information Economy*, Oxford University Press, New York, NY.

Bolisani E. and Scarso E. (1999) Information technology management: a knowledge-based perspective. *Technovation* **19**: 209-217.

Bontis N. (2001). Assessing knowledge assets: a review of the models used to measure intellectual capital. *International Journal of Management Reviews* **3**(1): 41-60.

Borghoff U. and Pareschi R. (1998). *Information Technology for Knowledge Management*. Springer-Verlag: Berlin.

Botkin J. (1999). *Smart Business: How Knowledge Communities Can Revolutionize Your Company*, Free Press, New York, NY.

Bradshaw R., Carpenter J., Cranfill R., Jeffers R., Poblete L., Robinson T., Sun A., Gawdiak Y., Bichindartz J. and Sullivan K. (1998). Roles for agent technology in knowledge management: examples from applications in aerospace and medicine. *Boeing Information and Support Services*: Seattle, WA.

Bramhall R. (1999). Knowledge management: what is it? *darkwing.uoregon.edu/~rbramhal/homepage/knowledge.html*

Brown J.S. and Duguid P. (2000). Balancing act: how to capture knowledge without killing it. *Harvard Business Review*: 73-80.

Bryman A. and Bell E. (2003). *Business Research Methods*. Oxford University Press: Oxford.

Buckley P.J. and Carter M.J. (2002). Process and structure in knowledge management practices of British and US multinational enterprises. *Journal of International Management* **8**(1): 29-48.

Burn J.M. and Ash C. (2000). Knowledge management strategies for virtual organisations. *Information Resources Management Journal,* Jan-Mar **13**(1): 15-23.

Business editors (2000). Ernst & Young intranet site recognised for excellence. *Business Wire.* www.findarticles.com/p1/article.html

Butler T. (2003). From data to knowledge and back again: understanding the limitations of KMS. *Knowledge and Process Management* **10**(3): 144-155.

Carlisle Y. (2000). Strategic thinking and knowledge management. In: Little S., Quintas P. and Ray T. (Ed) *Managing Knowledge: an Essential Reader*, Sage Publication: London:122-138.

Carlsson S.A., EI Sawy O.A., et al. (1996) Gaining competitive advantage through shared knowledge creation: in search of a new design theory for strategic information systems, In: *Proceedings of the Fourth European Conference on Information Systems*, Lisbon.

Carnelley P., Woods E., Vaughan D., et al. (2001) *Ovum Forecasts: Global Software Markets*, Ovum.

Cavalieri S. and Seivert S. (2005). *Knowledge Leadership: the Art and Science of Knowledge-Based Organization.* Elsevier Butterworth-Heinemann: Burlington, MA.

Cecez-Kecmanovic D. (2004). A sensemaking model of knowledge in organizations: a way of understanding knowledge management and the role of IT. *Knowledge Management Research & Practice.***2**:155-168

Cepeda G. (2006) Competitive advantage of knowledge management. In: Schwartz D.G (Ed.), *Encyclopedia of Knowledge Management.* Idea Group Reference: Hershey, PA: 34-43.

Chauvel D. and Desprs C. (2002) A review of survey research in knowledge management: 1997-2001. *Journal of Knowledge Management* **6**(3): 207-223.

Choo C.W. (1998a). Sharing knowledge through BP's virtual team network. *choo.fis.utoronto.ca/iss/km/KC.BP.html.*

Choo C.W. (1998b) *The Knowing Organization.* Oxford University Press: New York.

CIO Communications (1999). Knowledge management: big challenges, big rewards. CIO Special Advertising Supplement, *www.cio.com/sponsors/091599_km_1.html.*

Civi E. (2000). Knowledge management as a competitive asset: a review, *Marketing Intelligence & Planning*, **18**(4): 166-174.

Coakes S.J. (2005) *SPSS: Analysis Without Anguish: Version 12.0 for Window.* John Wiley & Sons Australia.

Collins H. (1993) The structure of knowledge. *Social Research* **60**: 95-116.

Cooper D.R. and Emory C.W. (1995). *Business Research Method, fifth edition.* Richard D. Irwin Inc.

Corbetta P. (2003). *Social Research: Theory, Methods and Techniques.* SAGE Publications: London.

Creswell J. (1994). *Research Design: Quantitative and Qualitative Approaches.* Sage: Thousand Oaks, CA.

Crossan M., Lane H., and White R. (1999). An organizational learning framework: from institution to institution. *Academy of Management Review* 24:522-538.

Crowely A. (1998). General Electric brings good things to web. *www.zdnet.com/eweek/fasttrack98/ge.html.*

Dalkir K. (2005). *Knowledge management in theory and practice.* Elsvier Butterworth-Heinemann, Burlington, MA

Damm D. and Schindler M. (2002). Security issues of a knowledge medium for distributed project work. *International Journal of Project Management* **20**(1): 37-47.

Dataquest (1999). Leveraging expertise: people-finder systems. *www.dqindia.com/mar3099/sps.htm.*

Davenport T.H. (1996). Hewlett-Packard promotes knowledge management initiatives.

Davenport T.H. (1997a). Knowledge management at Ernst & Young. *www.bus.utexas.edu/kman/e_y.html*

Davenport T.H. (1997b). *Information Ecology: Mastering the Information and Knowledge Environment.* Oxford University Press: New York.

Davenport T.H., DeLong D. and Beers M. (1998). Successful knowledge management projects. *Sloan Management Review* **39**(2): 43-57.

Davenport T.H. (1999). From data to knowledge, *CIO* **26**

Davenport T.H. and Prusak L. (2000). *Working Knowledge: How Organizations Manage What They Know. paperback edition.* Harvard Business School Press: Boston, Mass.

Davenport T.H. and Probst G.J.B. (2002). *Knowledge Management Case Book: Siemens Best Practices. second edition.* John Wiley & Sons: Berlin and Munich.

Dawes M. and Sampson U. (2003). Knowledge management in clinical practice: a systematic review of information seeking behavior in physicians. *International Journal of Medical Informatics* **71**: 9-15.

Dayasindhu N. (2002). Embeddedness, knowledge transfer, industry clusters and global competitiveness: a case study of the Indian software industry. *Technovation* **22**(9): 551-560.

Demarest M. (1997) Understanding knowledge management. *Long Range Planning* **30**(3): 374-384

Desouza K.C. (2003a). Barriers to effective use of knowledge management systems in software engineering. *Communications of the ACM*, January **46**(1): 99-101.

Desouza K.C. (2003b). Knowledge management barriers: Why the technology imperative seldom works. *Business Horizons*, January-February: 25-29.

Desouza K.C. (2003c). Facilitating tacit knowledge exchange. *Communications of the ACM*, June **46**(6): 85-88.

Detienne K.B. and Jackson L.A. (2001). Knowledge management: understanding theory and developing strategy. *Competitiveness Review*. **11**(1): 1-11.

Detlor B. (2000). The corporate portal as information infrastructure: towards a framework for portal design. *International Journal of Information Management* **20**(2): 91-101.

Dias C. (2001). Corporate portals: a literature review of a new concept in information management. *International Journal of Information Management* **21**: 269-287.

Douglas P.H. (2002). Information technology is out – knowledge sharing is in. *The Journal of Corporate Accounting & Finance*, May/June **13**(4): 73-77.

Drayton S. (1999). Knowledge management. AIOPI Information Forum, UK. *www.aiopi.org.uk/reports/99-km.htm.*

Dretske F. (1981). *Knowledge and the Flow of Information.* MIT Press: Cambridge, MA.

Drucker P.F. (1988). The coming of the new organization. *Harvard Business Review*, January-February: 45-53.

Drucker P.F. (1993). *Post Capitalist Society.* Harper Row: New York, NY.

Drucker P.F. (1997). The future that has already happened. *Harvard Business Review*, September-October: 20-24.

Dyer G. (2000). KM crosses the chasm: IDC state of the market survey. *Knowledge Management*, March: 50-54.

Earl M. (2001). Knowledge management strategies: Toward a taxonomy. *Journal of Management Information Systems,* Summer **18**(1): 215-233.

Easterby-Smith M., Thorpe R. and Lowe A. (1991). *Management Research: an Introduction.* Sage: London.

Ein-Dor P. (2006). Taxonomies of knowledge. In: Schwartz D.G. (Ed.), *Encyclopedia of Knowledge Management*, Idea Group Reference: Hershey, PA: 848-854.

Ernst & Young (1997). Knowledge Management: Research Report.

Fahey L. and Prusak L. (1998). The eleven deadliest sins of knowledge management. *California Management Review* 40(3): 265-276.

Fayyad U., Piatetsky-Shapiro G. and Smyth P. (1996). From data mining to knowledge discovery: an overview. In: Fayyad U. and Piatetsky-Shapiro G. (Eds.), *Advances in Knowledge Discovery and Data Mining*, MIT Press: Boston, MA: 1–34.

Fernandes K., Raja J.V. and Austin S. (2004). Portals as a knowledge repository and transfer tool—VIZCon case study. *Technovation*, April.

Fischer G. and Ostwald J. (2001). Knowledge management: problems, promises, realities, and challenges. *IEEE Intelligent Systems*, January/February: 60-72.

Firestone J.M. and McElroy M.W. (2003) *Key Issues in the New Knowledge Management*. Burlington, MA: KMCI Press/Butterworthe Heinemann

Firestone J.M. and McElroy M.W. (2005) Doing knowledge management. *The Learning Organization Journal*, **12**(2)

Fleck J. (1997). Contingent knowledge and technology development. *Technology Analysis & Strategic Management* **9**(4): 383-397.

Foy P.S. (1999). Knowledge management in industry. In: Liebowitz J. (Ed), *Knowledge Management Handbook*. CRC Press.

Frawley W.J., Piatetsky-Shapiro G. and Matheus C.J. (1992). Knowledge discovery in databases: an overview. *AI Magazine* **13** (3): 57–70.

Fryer B. (1999). Get smart. *www.inc.com/incmagazine/articles/details/print*

Gandhi S. (2004). Knowledge management and reference services. *The Journal of Academic Librarianship,* September 30(5): 368-381.

Gao F., Li M. and Nakamori Y. (2002). Systems thinking on knowledge and its management: systems methodology for knowledge management. *Journal Of Knowledge Management* 6(1):7-17.

Garavelli A.C., Gorgoglione M. and Scozzi B. (2002). Managing knowledge transfer by knowledge technologies. *Technovation* **22**(5): 269-279.

Gartner Group (1998). Knowledge management scenario. Conference presentation.

Garvin D.A. (1993). Building a learning organization. *Harvard Business Review* **71**(4): 78-91.

Gazeau M. (1998). Le Management de la Connaissance. Etats de Veille, Juin: 1-8.

Germain R., Droge C., et al. (2001). The mediating role of operations knowledge in the relationship of context with performance. *Journal of Operations Management* **19**(4): 453-469.

Godbout A.J. (1999). State of the knowledge management art: lessons learned from early adoptions of knowledge management. *www.magi.com/~godbout/Kbase/td99103.html.*

Gordon J., Niinuma K., Rajaran G. and Sherman S. (1998). Buckman Laboratories International, *www.bus.utexas.edu/kmrg/Team305/buckman.html.*

Grant R. (1991). The resource-based theory of competitive advantage: implications for strategy formulation. *California Management Review* **33**(3): 114-135.

Grant R. (1996). Towards a knowledge-based theory of the firm. *Strategic Management Journal* **17** Spring: 109-122.

Gray P.H. (2001) A problem-solving perspective on knowledge management practices. *Decision Support Systems* **31**: 87–102

Gray P. and Tehrani S. (2003) Technology for disseminating knowledge. In: Holsapple C.W. (Ed.), *Handbook on knowledge management 2 knowledge directions.* Springer: Heidelberg: 110-127.

Gunnlaugsdottir J. (2003). Seek and you will find, share and you will benefit: organising knowledge using groupware systems. *International Journal of Information Management* **23**: 363–380.

Hakim C. (1982). *Secondary Analysis in Social Research.* Allen&Unwin: London.

Hall R. (2003). *Knowledge Management in the New Business Environment*, Australian Centre for Industrial Relations Research & Training, University of Sydney, Australian Business Foundation.

Hansen M.T., Nohria N. and Tierney T. (1999). What's your strategy for managing knowledge? *Harvard Business Review* **77**(2): 106–116.

Hasan H. and Crawford K. (2003). Codifying or enabling: the challenge of knowledge management systems. *Journal of the Operational Research Society* **54**: 184-193.

Hasanali F. and Leavitt P. (2003). *Content Management: A Guide for Your Journey to Knowledge Management Best Practices.* American Productivity and Quality Center.

Hendriks P.H.J. (2001). Many rivers to cross: from ICT to knowledge management systems. *Journal of information technology* **16**: 57-72

Heinrichs J.H. and Lim J.-S. (2003). Integrating web-based data mining tools with business models for knowledge management. *Decision Support Systems* **35**:103–112.

Hendriks P.H.J. (2006). Organizational structure. In: Schwartz D.G. (Ed.), *Encyclopedia of Knowledge Management,* Idea Group Reference: Hershey, PA: 749-756.

Hibbard J. (1997). Knowing what we know. *Information Week* **653**: 46-64.

Hiscock J. (2004). Developing knowledge management awareness in public relations students. *Public Relations Review* **30**(1): 107-115.

Holsapple C.W. and Joshi D. (1998). In search of a descriptive framework for knowledge management: preliminary Delphi results. Kentucky Initiative for Knowledge Management.

Holsapple C.W. and Joshi D. (2000). Understanding knowledge management solution: the evolution of frameworks in theory and practice. In: Barnes S. (Ed.), *Knowledge Management Systems: Theory and Practice,* Thomson Learning: London, 222-241.

Holsapple C.W. and Jones K. (2006). Knowledge management strategy formation. In Schwartz D.G. (Ed.), *Encyclopedia of knowledge management*, Idea Group Reference: Hershey, PA: 419-428.

Holtshouse D. (2000). Ten knowledge domains – model of a knowledge-driven company. Montgomery Research Inc. *hotshouse.crmproject.com.*

Housel T. and Bell A.H. (2001). *Measuring and Managing Knowledge*. MacGraw-Hill/Irwin: New York, NY.

Huang, K. T. (1998). Capitalizing on intellectual assets, *IBM Systems Journal* **37**(4). *www.resesarch.ibm.com/journal/sj/374/huang.html.*

Huber G.P. (2001). Transfer of knowledge in knowledge management systems: unexplored issues and suggested studies. *European Journal of Information Systems* **10**: 72-79.

Hupic V., Pouloudi A. and Rzevski G. (2002). Towards an integrated approach to knowledge management: 'hard', 'soft' and 'abstract' issues. *Knowledge and Process Management* **9**(2): 90-102.

Huysman M., Creamers M. and Derksen D. (1998). Learning from the Environment: Exploring the Relation between Organizational Learning, Knowledge Management and Information/ Communication Technology. In: Hoadley E. and Benbasat I. (Eds.), *Proceedings of the Fourth Americas Conference on Information Systems*, Baltimore, MD, August: 598-600.

Information services advisory council (1998). Managing information as a strategic asset: corporate intranet development and the role of the company library. *www.conference-board.org/products/intranet-white-paper.cfm.*

Jackson C. (1999). Process to product – creating tools for knowledge management hype. *Journal for Quality and Participation* **21**(4): 58-60.

Jarke M. (2002). Experience-based knowledge management: a cooperative information systems perspective. *Control Engineering Practice* **10**(5): 561-569.

Jarrar Y.F. (2002) Knowledge management: learning for organisational experience, *Managerial Auditing Journal* **17**(6): 322-328

Jennex M. (2006) Knowledge management success factors. In: Schwartz D.G. (Ed.), *Encyclopedia of Knowledge Management*, Idea Group Reference: Hershey, PA: 436-441.

Johannessen J.-A., Olaisen J. and Olsen B. (2001). Mismanagement of tacit knowledge: the importance of tacit knowledge, the danger of information technology, and what to do about it. *International Journal of Information Management* **21**:3-20.

Junnarkar B. and Brown C.V. (1997). Re-assessing the enabling role of information technology in KM. *Journal of Knowledge Management,* December **1**(2).

Kakabadse N.K., Kakabadse A. and Kouzmin A. (2003). Reviewing the knowledge management literature: towards a taxonomy. *Journal of Knowledge Management* **7**(4): 75-91.

Kamara J.M., Anumba C.J. and Carrillo P.M. (2002). A CLEVER approach to selecting a knowledge management strategy. *International Journal of Project Management* **20**(3): 205-211.

Kankanhalli A., Tanudidjaja F., Sutanto J. and Tan B.C.Y. (2003). The role of IT in successful knowledge management initiatives, *Communications of the ACM,* September **46**(9): 69-73.

Kanter J. (1999). Knowledge management practically speaking, *Information Systems Management,* **Fall**: 7-15.

Kaplan R.S. and Norton D.P. (1996) *The Balanced Scoreboard.* Harvard Business School Press: Boston, MA

Klobas J. E. (1997). Information services for new millennium organisations: Librarians and knowledge management, In: Raitt D. (Ed.), *Libraries for the New Millennium: Implications for Managers.* Library Association: London: 39–64.

Koch H., Paradice D., Chae B. and Guo Y. (2002). An investigation of knowledge management within a university IT group. *Information Resources Management Journal,* Jan-Mar, **15**(1): 13-21.

KPMG Management Consulting. (1998a). *Case Study: Building a Platform for Corporate Knowledge.*

KPMG Management Consulting (1998b). *Knowledge Management: Research Report.*

KPMG Management Consulting. (2000). *Knowledge Management Report.*

Kulkarni U. and Freeze R. (2006). Measuring knowledge management capabilities. In: Schwartz D.G. (Ed.), *Encyclopedia of Knowledge Management.* Idea Group Reference: Hershey, PA: 605-613.

Lang C.J. (2001). Managerial concerns in knowledge management. *Journal of Knowledge Management* **5**(1): 43-57.

Lawton G. (2001). Knowledge management: ready for prime time? *Computer* **34**(2): 12-14.

Lee J.-N. and Kwok R.C.-W. (2000). A fuzzy GSS framework for organizational knowledge acquisition. *International Journal of Information Management* **20**(5): 383-398.

Lehaney B., Clarke S., Coakes E. and Jack G. (2004). *Beyond Knowledge Management.* Idea Group Publishing: Hershey, PA.

Leonard D. (1999). *Wellsprings of Knowledge: Building and Sustaining the Sources of Innovation*, Harvard Business School Press: Boston, MA.

Lewis D. (1998). Dying for information? *Reuters Business Information*

Liao S.H. (2002). Problem solving and knowledge inertia. *Expert Systems with Applications* **22**(1): 21-31.

Liao S.H. (2003) Knowledge management technologies and applications—literature review from 1995 to 2002. *Expert Systems with Applications*, August **25** (2) 155–164.

Liebowittz J. (1999). *Knowledge Management Handbook*, CRC Press: London.

Liebowitz J. (2001). Knowledge management and its links to artificial intelligence. *Expert Systems With Applications* **20**:1-6.

Liebowitz J. and Megbolugbe I. (2003). A set of frameworks to aid the project manager in conceptualizing and implementing knowledge management initiatives. *International Journal of Project Management* **21**(3): 189-198.

Liew C.L. and Foo S. (1999). Derivation of interaction environment and information object properties for enhanced integrated access and value-adding to electronic documents. *Aslib Proceedings.* September, **51** (8): 256-268

Lueg C. (2001). Information, knowledge, and networked minds. *Journal of Knowledge Management* **5**(2): 151-159.

Lundvall B.A. (1996). *The Social Dimension of the Learning Economy.* Department of business studies, Aalborg University, Denmark.

Machlup F. (1980). *Knowledge: Its Creation, Distribution, and Economic Significance, Volume I.* Princeton University Press: Princeton, NJ.

Mack R., Ravin Y. and Byrd R.J. (2001). Knowledge portals and the emerging digital knowledge workplace. *IBM Systems Journal* **40**(4): 925-955.

Maier R. and Lehner F. (2000). Perspectives on knowledge management systems theoretical framework and design of an empirical study. In: *Proceedings of 8th European Conference on Information Systems (ECIS).*

Maier R. and Remus U. (2002). Defining process-oriented knowledge management strategies. *Knowledge and Process Management* **9**(2): 103-108.

Maier R. and Remus U. (2003). Implementing process-oriented knowledge management strategies. *Journal of Knowledge Management* **7**(4): 62-74.

Maier R. (2004). *Knowledge Management Systems: Information and Communication Technologies for Knowledge Management, second edition.* Springer: Berlin.

Maier R. and Hadrich T. (2006). Knowledge management systems. In: Schwartz D.G. (Ed.), *Encyclopedia of Knowledge Management.* Idea Group Reference: Hershey, PA: 442-450.

Malafsky G.P. (2003). Technology for acquiring and sharing knowledge assets. In: Holsapple C.W. (Ed.), *Handbook on Knowledge Management 2 Knowledge Directions.* Springer: Heidelberg: 85-107.

Malhotra Y. (1999). From information management to knowledge management: Beyond the "Hi-Tech Hidebound" systems. In: Malhotra Y. (Ed.), *Knowledge Management and Business Model Innovation*, Idea Group Publishing: Hershey, PA: 115-134.

Malhotra Y. (2000). Towards a knowledge ecology for organizational knowledge management. *www.brint.com.*

Malhotra Y. (2002). Why knowledge management systems fail? Enablers and constraints of knowledge management in human enterprises. *http://www.yogeshmalhotra.com.*

Manual (2004). Manual for PQM knowledge portal. Internal document.

Martensson, M. (2000). A critical review of knowledge management as a management tool. *Journal of Knowledge Management* **4**(3): 204-216.

Martin W.J. (2004). Demonstrating knowledge value: a broader perspective on metrics, *Journal of Intellectual Capital* **5**(1): 77-91.

Martin W.J. (2007). Knowledge management, *Annual review of information science and technology* **42**, Fall.

Marwick A.D. (2001). Knowledge management technology. *IBM Systems Journal: Knowledge Management* **40**(4).

McAdam R. and McMreedy S. (1999). A critical review of knowledge management models. *The Learning Organization* **6**(3): 91-100.

McDermott R. (1999). Why information technology inspired but cannot deliver knowledge management. *California Management Review,* Summer **41**(1): 103-117.

McNamara C., Baxter J. et al. (2004). Making and managing organisational knowledge(s). *Management Accounting Research* **15**(1): 53-76.

McQueen R. (1998). Four Views of Knowledge and Knowledge Management, In: *Proceedings of the Fourth Americas Conference on Information Systems*, August: 609-611.

Mentzas G. et al. (2001). Knowledge networking: a holistic solution for leveraging corporate knowledge. *Journal of Knowledge Management* **5**(1): 94-106.

Merlyn P. and Valikangas L. (1998). From information technology to knowledge technology: taking the user into consideration. *Journal of Knowledge Management* **2**(2): 28-35.

Mertins K., Heisig P. and Vobeck J. (2001). *Knowledge management: best practices in Europe*. Springer-Verlag: Berlin.

Meso P. and Smith R. (2000). A resource-based view of organizational knowledge management systems. *Journal of Knowledge Management* **4**(3): 224-234.

Meyer M. and Zack H.M. (1996). The design and implementation of information products, *Sloan Management Review* **37**(3): 43-59.

Millar J., Demaid A. and Quintas P. (1997). Trans-organisational innovation: a framework for research. *Technology Analysis & Strategic Management* **9**(4): 399-418.

Miller W. (1996). Capitalizing on knowledge relationships with customers. In: *Proceedings, knowledge management '96*. Business Intelligence Inc. London.

Mo J.P.T. and Zhou M. (2003). Tools and methods for managing intangible assets of virtual enterprise. *Computers in Industry* **51**(2): 197-210.

Moffett S., McAdam R. and Parkinson S. (2003). Technology and people factors in knowledge management: an empirical analysis. *Total Quality Management* **14**(2): 215-224.

Morris T. and Wood S. (1991). Testing the survey method: continuity and change in British industrial relations. *Work Employment and Society*, **5**(2): 259-282.

Musgrave A. (1993). *Common Sense, Science and Scepticism*. Cambridge University Press: Cambridage.

Myers, P.S. (1999). *Making the business case for knowledge management*. Boston: ICEX. *www.icex.com.*

Ndlela L.T. and Toit A. (2001). Establishing a knowledge management programme for competitive advantage in an enterprise. *International Journal of Information Management* **21**(2): 151-165.

Nemati H.R., Steiger D.M., Iyer L.S. and Herschel R.T. (2002). Knowledge warehouse: an architectural integration of knowledge management, decision support, artificial intelligence and data warehousing. *Decision Support Systems* **33**(2): 143-161.

Neuman W.L. (1994). *Social Research Methods: Qualitative and Quantitative Approaches.* Allyn and Bacon: MA.

Nevis E., DiBella A. and Gold J. (1995). Understanding organizations as learning systems. *Sloan Management Review* Winter, 73-85.

Nidumolo S., Subramani M., and Aldrich A. (2005) Situated learning and situated knowledge web: exploring the ground beneath knowledge management. *Journal of Management InformationSystem* Summer, **18**(1): 115-150.

Nissen M.E. (2006). Harnessing knowledge dynamics: principled organizational knowing & learning. IRM Press: Hershey PA

Nonaka I. (1994). A dynamic theory of organizational knowledge creation. *Organization Science,* February, **5**(1): 14-37.

Nonaka I. and Takeuchi H. (1995). *The Knowledge-Creating Company: How Japanese Companies Create the Dynamics of Innovation.* Oxford University Press: New York.

O'Dell C. and Grayson C.J. (1998). If only we knew what we know: identification and transfer of internal best practices. *California Management Review* **40** (3): 154-174.

O'Dell C., Hasanali F., Hubert C., Lopez K., Odem P. and Raybourn C. (2003). Successful KM implementation: a study of best-practice organizations. In: Holsapple C.W. (Ed.), *Handbook on Knowledge Management 2 Knowledge Directions.* Springer: Heidelberg: 411-441.

OECD (1996). *Knowledge-based Economy,* Paper presented at the OECD, Paris.

Offsey S. (1997) Knowledge management: linking people to knowledge for bottom line results. *Journal of Knowledge Management* December, **1**(2): 113-122.

Ogden P. (1998). Comment: Benchmarking and best practice in the small hotel sector. *International Journal of Contemporary Hospitality Management* **10**(5): 189-190.

O'Leary D.E. and Studer R. (2001). Knowledge management: an interdisciplinary approach. *IEEE Intelligent Systems,* January/February: 24-25.

Ordonez de Pablos P. (2002). Knowledge management and organizational learning: typologies of knowledge strategies in the Spanish manufacturing industry from 1995 to 1999. *Journal of Knowledge Management* **6**(1): 52-62.

Pan, S.L. and Leidner, D.E. (2003). Bridging communities of practice with information technology in pursuit of global knowledge sharing. *Journal of Strategic Information Systems* **12**: 71–88.

Parlby D. (1997). *The Power of Knowledge: A Business Guide to Knowledge Management.* KPMG Management Consulting, Internal report.

Pearlson K.E. and Saunders C.S. (2006) Managing & using information systems: a strategic approach. Third Edition. John Wiley & Sons.

Pedersen M.K. and Larsen M.H. (2001). Distributed knowledge management based on product state models -- the case of decision support in health care administration. *Decision Support Systems* **31**(1): 139-158.

Pickering J.M. and King J.L. (1995). Hardwiring weak ties: Interorganizational computer-mediated communication, occupational communities, and organizational change. *Organization Science* **6**(4): 479-486.

Plessis M. (2005). Drivers of knowledge management in the corporate environment. *International Journal of Information Management* **25**: 193-202.

Polanyi M. (1983). *The tacit dimension.* Peter Smith reprint: Gloucester, MA.

PQM manual (2002). Program quality management manual. *www.rmit.edu.au/our organisation/ chancellery/planning group/information and services/quality.*

Prahalad C.K. and Hamel G. (1990). The core competence of the corporation. *Harvard Business Review* **68**(3):79-93.

Prat N. (2006). A hierachical model for knowledge management, In: Schwartz D.G. (Ed.), *Encyclopedia of Knowledge Management*. Idea Group Reference: Hershey, PA: 848-854.

PRNewswire (2000). Knowledge management: driving corporate learning and growth, PRNewswire, *www.findarticles.com/m4PRN/*

Prusak L. (2006). Foreword. In: Schwartz D.G. (Ed.), *Encyclopaedia of Knowledge Management*, Idea Group Reference: Hershey, PA.

Purvis R.L., Sambamurthy V. and Zmud R.W. (2001). The assimilation of knowledge platforms in organizations: an empirical investigation. *Organization Science* **12**: 117-135.

Remenyi D., Williams B., Money A. and Swartz E. (1998). *Doing Research in Business and Management: An Introduction to Process and Method,* Sage: London.

Reyes P. and Raisinghani M.S. (2002). Integrating information technologies and knowledge-based systems: a theoretical approach in action for enhancements in production and inventory control, *Knowledge and Process Management* **9**(4): 256-263.

Roberts J. (2000). From know-how to show-how: questioning the role of information and communication technologies in knowledge transfer. *Technology Analysis & Strategic Management* **12**(4).

Robson C. (1993). *Real World Research: A Resource for Social Scientist and Practitioner - Researchers.* Blackwell: Oxford.

Rollo C. and Clarke T. (2001). *Knowledge Management Case Studies*. Standards Australia: Sydney.

Romano A., Elia V. and Passiante G. (2001). Creating business innovation leadership. An ongoing experiment: the e-business management school at ISUFI. Edizioni Scintifiche Italiane.

Roos G. and Roos J. (1997). Measuring your company's intellectual performance, *Long Range Planning* **30**(3): 413-427.

Rosen I. (1998) Capturing and sharing competitive intelligence: Microsoft's intranet, *www.scip.org/news/cimagazine_article.html*

Rothfinder J. (1999). Known quantity: the merger that created PricewaterhouseCoopers could have wreaked havoc on the company's knowledge-management infrastructure. *www.ee-online.com/dec.*

Rowley J. (1999). What is knowledge management? *Library management.* **20**(8): 416-419.

Ruggles R. (1998). The state of the notion: knowledge management in practice. *California Management Review* **40**: 80–89.

Russ M., Jones J. and Fineman R. (2006). Towards a taxonomy of knowledge-based strategies: early findings. *International Journal of Knowledge and Learning* **2**(1/2): 1-40.

Saunders M., Lewis P. and Thornhill A. (2000). *Research Methods for Business Students. second edition.* Pearson Education. Essex England

Schultze U. (1999). Investigating the contradictions in knowledge management. In: Larsen T.J., Levine L., and De Gross J.I. (Eds.), *Information systems: current issues and future changes.* IFIP,Laxenberg, Austria:155-174.

Schultze U. and Boland R. (2000). Knowledge management technology and the reproduction of knowledge work practices. *Journal strategic information systems* **9**: 193-212.

Schultze U. and Leidner D.E. (2002) Studying knowledge management in information systems research: discourses and theoretical assumptions. *MIS Quarterly* **26**(3): 213-242.

Schwartz P., Eamonn K. and Boyer N. (1999). The emerging global knowledge economy. In: OECD, *The future of the global economy: towards a long boom.*

Scott J.E. (1998). Organizational knowledge and the Intranet. *Decision Support Systems* 23: 3–17

Shaw M.J., Subramaniam C., Tan, G.W. and Welge M.E. (2001) Knowledge management and data mining for marketing. *Decision Support Systems* **31**:127–137.

Sher P.J. and Lee V.C. (2003) Information technology as a facilitator for enhancing dynamic capabilities through knowledge management. *Information & Management*

Shin M., Holden T. and Schmidt R.A. (2001). From knowledge theory to management practice: towards an integrated approach. *Information Processing and Management.* **37**: 335-355.

Singh H., Bowman E.H. and Kale P. (1999). Building alliance capacity. 1999 Midyear industry partner meeting, Pennsylvania.
emertech.wharton.upenn.edu/emertech/ConfRpts_folder/cfKnowFlo

Smith H. (1975). *Strategies of Social Research: The Methodological Imagination.* Prentic-Hall: Englewood cliffs, NJ.

Snowden D.J. (2000). Cynefin: a sense of time and space, the social ecology of knowledge management. In: Despres C. & Chauvel D. (Ed.) *Knowledge horizons: the present and the promise of knowledge management* Boston, Butterworth-Heinemann: 237-265

Snowden D.J. (2002). Complex acts of knowing: paradox and descriptive self-awareness, *Journal of Knowledge Management* **6**(2): 1-14

Song H., Martin B. and Deng H. (2003). A novel model for integrating organizational data, information and knowledge in effective knowledge management. In: *Proceedings of the Fourth International Conference on Intelligent Technologies.* Chiang Mei.

Song H., Deng H. and Martin B. (2004). Towards a pragmatic approach to knowledge management: a multi-perspectives analysis. In: *Proceedings of the Second International Conference on Knowledge Economy and Development of Science and Technologies.* Beijing.

Song H. and Deng H. (2005). Technological approach to knowledge management. In: *Proceedings of the Second International conference on Information Management and Science.* Kunming.

Song H., Deng H. and Martin B. (2006). Sharing information and knowledge through the application of information and communication technologies: an empirical study. In: *The Fifth International Conference on Information Management and Science.* Chengdu.

Song J., Almeida P. and Wu G. (2003). Learning-by-hiring: when is mobility more likely to facilitate interfirm knowledge transfer? *Management Science* April **49**: 351-366

Sorenson O. (2003). Interdependence and adaptability: organizational learning and the long-term effect of integration. *Management Science* April **49**:446-464.

Spender J. (1996). Making knowledge the basis of a dynamic theory of the firm. *Strategic Management Journal* Winter **17**: 45-62.

Spiegler I. (2003). Technology and knowledge: bridging a "generating" gap. *Information & Management* **40**(6): 533-539.

Stephenson Strategies (2000). Case studies: US Army & Xerox. *www.stephensonstrategies.com/intranet_strategy/week_five/ case_studies.html*

Stromquist N. and Samoff J. (2000). Knowledge management systems: on the promise and actual forms of information technologies. *Compare* **30**(3): 323-332.

Sveiby K.E. (1997). *The New Organizational Wealth: Managing and Measuring Knowledge-Based Assets*. Brrett-Koeher: San Francisco, CA.

Sveiby K.E. (1999). Knowledge management. *www.knowledgecreators.com/km/kes/kes27.htm*.

Swan J. (2001). Knowledge management in action: integrating knowledge across communities. In: *Proceedings of the 32nd Annual Hawaii International Conference on System Sciences*.

Tan S.S., Teo H.H., et al. (1998). Developing a preliminary framework for knowledge management in organizations. In: Hoadley E. and Benbasat I. (Eds.), *Proceedings of the Fourth Americas Conference on Information Systems*, August: 629-631. Baltimore, MD.

Tan X., Yen D.C. and Fang X. (2003). Web warehousing: Web technology meets data warehousing. *Technology in Society* **25**: 131–148

Teece D. (1998). Capturing value from knowledge assets: the new economy, markets for know-how, and intangible assets. *California Management Review* **40**(3): 55-79.

Telang R. and Mukhopadhyay T. (2005). Drivers of web portal use. *Electronic Commerce Research and Applications* **4**: 49-65.

Teleos (2004). 2004 Global Most Admired Knowledge Enterprises (MAKE) Report Executive Summary. *www.knowledgebusiness.com*

Teleos (2005). 2005 Global Most Admired Knowledge Enterprises (MAKE) Report Executive Summary. *www.knowledgebusiness.com*

Teleos (2006), 2006 Global Most Admired Knowledge Enterprises (MAKE) Report Executive Summary. *www.knowledgebusiness.com*

Teo T.S.H. (2005). Meeting the challenges of knowledge management at the Housing and Development Board. *Decision Support Systems* **41**: 147–159.

Ticehurst G.W. and Veal A.J. (2000) *Business Research Methods: A Managerial Approach.* Pearson Eduction Australia: NSW.

Tierney T. and Bain & Co (1999). What's your strategy for managing knowledge? *www.cstp.umkc.edu/~place/courses/EMBA/Sections/Orgnization_Chg.*

Tsui E. (2000). Exploring the KM toolbox, *Knowledge Management* **4**(2): 11-14.

Tsui E. (2003). Tracking the role and evolution of commercial Knowledge Management software, In: Holsapple C.W. (Ed.), *Handbook on Knowledge Management*, Springer: Heidelberg: 5-25.

Tsui E. (2005). The role of IT in KM: where are we now and where are we heading? *Journal of Knowledge Management* **9**(1): 3-6.

Tuomi I. (2000). Data is more than knowledge: implications of the reversed hierarchy for knowledge management and organizational memory. *Journal of Management Information Systems* **16**(3): 103-117.

Turban E., Mclean E. and Wetherbe J. (1999). *Information Technology for Management: Making Connections for Strategic Advantages*, Wiley: New York.

Turban E., Lee J., King D. and Chung H.M. (2000). *Electronic Commerce: A Managerial Perspective*. Prentice Hall: Upper saddle river, NJ.

Tyndale P. (2002). A taxonomy of knowledge management software tools: origins and applications. *Evaluation and Program Planning* **25**: 83-190.

University annual report (2005). University annual report. *www.rmit.edu.au/about/ publications#annual.*

Vance D.M. (1997). Information, knowledge and wisdom: the epistemic hierarchy and computer-based information system. In: Perkins B. and Vessey I. (Eds.), *Proceedings of the Third Americas Conference on Information Systems*, Indianapolis, IN, August.

Van der Spek R. and Spijkervet A. (1997). Knowledge management: dealing intelligently with knowledge. In: Liebowitz J. and Wilcox (Eds.) *Knowledge and its Intergrative Elements*. CRC Press: New York.

Walsham G. (2001). Knowledge management: the benefits and limitations of computer systems. *European Management Journal* December, **19**(6): 599-608.

Wang S. and Ariguzo G. (2004). Knowledge management through the development of information schema. *Information & Management* **41**(4): 445-456.

Watson J. and Fenner J. (2000). Understanding portals. *Information Management Journal*, July, **34**(3): 18-22.

Wensley A. (2000). Tools for knowledge management. *BPRC Conference on knowledge management: concepts and controversies*, 10-11, February, Coventry, University of Warwick.

Wick C. (2000). Knowledge management and leadership opportunities for technical communicators. *Technical Communications*, November.

Wickramasinghe N. and Mills G.L. (2002). Integrating e-commerce and knowledge management--what does the Kaiser experience really tell us. *International Journal of Accounting Information Systems* **3**(2): 83-98.

Wickramasinghe N. (2003). Do we practise what we preach? *Business Process Management Journal* **9**(3): 295-316.

Wiig K.M. (1993). *Knowledge Management Foundations*. Schema Press: Arlington, VA.

Wiig K.M. (1997). Knowledge management: where did it come from and where will it go? *Expert Systems With Applications* **13**(1): 1-14.

Wijetunge P. (2002). Adoption of knowledge management by the Sri Lankan University librarians in the light of the national policy on university education. *International Journal of Educational Development* **22**(1): 85-94.

Wolford D. and Kwiecien S. (2003). Driving Knowledge Management at Ford Motor company. In: Holsapple C.W. (Ed.), *Handbook on Knowledge Management 2 Knowledge Directions*. Springer, Heidelberg: 501-510.

Woods E. and Sheina M. (1999). *Knowledge management: building the collaborative enterprise*, Ovum.

Yang J.-T. and Wan C.-S. (2004). Advancing organizational effectiveness and knowledge management implementation. *Tourism Management*.

Yim N., Kim S. et al. (2004) Knowledge based decision making on higher level strategic concerns: system dynamics approach. *Expert Systems with Applications*.

Yin R.K. (2003). *Case Study Research: Design and Methods. third edition*. Sage: California.

Zack M.H. (1998a). An architecture for managing explicated knowledge. *Sloan Management Review*, September.

Zack M.H. (1998b) What knowledge-problems can information technology help to solve. In: Hoadley E. and Benbasat I. (Eds.), *Proceedings of the Fourth Americas Conference on Information Systems*, Baltimore, MD, August: 644-646.

Zack M.H. (1999). *Knowledge and Strategy*. Butterworth Heinemann: Boston, MA.

Zack M.H. (2000). If managing knowledge is the solution, then what's the problem? In: Malhotra Y. (Ed.), *Knowledge Management and Business Model Innovation*, Idea Group Publishing: Hershey, PA: 16-36.

Zack M.H. (2002). Developing a knowledge strategy. In: Choo C. W. and Bontis N. (Ed.), *The Strategic Management of Intellectual Capital and Organizational Knowledge*, Oxford University Press: Oxford: 255-276.

Zeleny M. (2002). Knowledge of enterprise: knowledge management or knowledge technology? *International Journal of Information Technology & Decision Making* **1**(2): 181-207.

Zhang X. and Haslam M. (2005). Movement toward a predominantly electronic journal collection. *Library Hi Tech* **23**(1): 82-89.

Zobel C.W., Rees L.P., et al. (2004). Automated merging of conflicting knowledge bases, using a consistent, majority-rule approach with knowledge-form maintenance. *Computers & Operations Research*.

Appendix A
Questionnaire

Electronic Resource Survey

Electronic resource includes journals, newspapers, archives, theses, exam papers, government papers and other materials in electronic form. This survey is designed to investigate the use of electronic resource in library within the context of knowledge management. It aims to help users to take full advantage of electronic resource and help library provide better service relating to electronic resource.

Section 1:   Background

Q.1.   Which group do you belong to?
- ☐ Academic staff
- ☐ Administrative staff
- ☐ Postgraduate by course student
- ☐ Postgraduate by research student
- ☐ Undergraduate student
- ☐ TAFE student
- ☐ Others, please specify:
  _____

Q.2.   How many years have you been in current work/study position?
- ☐ 1
- ☐ 2
- ☐ 3
- ☐ 4
- ☐ 5-10
- ☐ 11-25
- ☐ 26-30
- ☐ More than 30

Q.3.   What is your age group?
- ☐ Under 20
- ☐ 20-29
- ☐ 30-39
- ☐ 40-49
- ☐ 50-59
- ☐ 60 and over

Q.4.   Currently, what is your highest level of education qualification?
- ☐ PhD or equivalent degree
- ☐ Master
- ☐ Bachelor
- ☐ Diploma
- ☐ Certificate
- ☐ Others, please specify:
  _____

Q.5.   What is your gender?
- ☐ Female ☐ Male

Section 2:   **Use of Electronic Resource**

Q.6.   Do you ever use electronic resource?
☐   Yes   ☐   No
If no, please go to Q29.

Q.7.   How do you access electronic resources?
☐   On-campus and within library
☐   On-campus and outside library
☐   Off-campus and on-shore
☐   Off-campus and off-shore

Q.8.   What electronic resources do you use?
☐   Library catalogue   ☐   Electronic exam paper   ☐   Online magazines
☐   Online journals   ☐   Website information   ☐   Others, please specify:
☐   Online theses   ☐   Electronic books   _____
☐   Online archive   ☐   Online newspapers

Q.9.   How often do you access electronic resource?
☐   More than once a week   ☐   Once a month
☐   Once a week   ☐   Less than once a month
☐   Once a fortnight   ☐   Never

Q.10.   What's the purpose when you use electronic resource?
☐   To gain general information
☐   To get answers to some specific questions
☐   To gather information on a specific topic
☐   To do the literature review
☐   To write an essay
☐   To make a decision
☐   To complete an assignment
☐   Others, please specify: _____

Q.11.   Why do you choose to use electronic resource?
☐   Ease to access
☐   Save time
☐   Without the physical space limitation
☐   Abundance
☐   Availability of search tools
☐   Others, please specify: _____

Q.12.   Have you ever taken any training course/ tutorial / guide to use electronic resource?
   ☐   Yes
   ☐   No

Section 3: Role of Electronic Resource

Q.13.   Is the use of electronic resource part of your work/study?
   ☐   Yes   ☐   No   ☐   No, but attempt to

Q.14.   Have you ever made your ideas available electronically in any way?
   ☐   Yes   ☐   No   ☐   No, but attempt to

Q.15.   Have you published any item of scholarship in electronic form?
   ☐   Yes   ☐   No   ☐   No, but attempt to

Q.16.   Have you integrated electronic resources into any of the tasks that you undertake?
   ☐   Yes   ☐   No   ☐   No, but attempt to

Q.17.   How do you rate that electronic resource helps you accomplish your task?
   ☐   extremely useful   ☐   not sure
   ☐   quite useful   ☐   not useful
   ☐   useful

Q.18.   In what situation do you find the electronic resource useful?
   ☐   To complete an assignment/essay/thesis/paper
   ☐   To undertake a research project
   ☐   To undergo a routine task
   ☐   To undergo a new task
   ☐   To make a simple decision
   ☐   To make a complex decision
   ☐   To gain new insights/ideas
   ☐   To compare the different views
   ☐   Others, please specify:_____

Section 4:   Impacting Factors

Do you agree the following statements?

Q.19.   What I find from electronic resource is not what I need.
   ☐   Strongly Agree   ☐   Agree   ☐   Neutral   ☐   Disagree   ☐   Strongly Disagree

Q.20.   There is too much electronic resource.
   ☐   Strongly Agree   ☐   Agree   ☐   Neutral   ☐   Disagree   ☐   Strongly Disagree

---

Q.21. Electronic resource is not updated.

☐ Strongly Agree ☐ Agree ☐ Neutral ☐ Disagree ☐ Strongly Disagree

Q.22. It takes too much time to find the relevant electronic resource.

☐ Strongly Agree ☐ Agree ☐ Neutral ☐ Disagree ☐ Strongly Disagree

Q.23. Lack of supporting equipment (such as connection, download, printing equipment) limits the use of electronic resource.

☐ Strongly Agree ☐ Agree ☐ Neutral ☐ Disagree ☐ Strongly Disagree

Q.24. Electronic resource is not always accessible.

☐ Strongly Agree ☐ Agree ☐ Neutral ☐ Disagree ☐ Strongly Disagree

Q.25. Guide/help/training to use electronic resource is not enough.

☐ Strongly Agree ☐ Agree ☐ Neutral ☐ Disagree ☐ Strongly Disagree

Q.26. More specific guide to use electronic resource related to topic/subtopic/ discipline/field I am interested in is needed.

☐ Strongly Agree ☐ Agree ☐ Neutral ☐ Disagree ☐ Strongly Disagree

Q.27. Examples and experiences on effective use of electronic resource are needed.

☐ Strongly Agree ☐ Agree ☐ Neutral ☐ Disagree ☐ Strongly Disagree

Q.28. Relevant electronic resource should be pushed based on the user profile and interest.

☐ Strongly Agree ☐ Agree ☐ Neutral ☐ Disagree ☐ Strongly Disagree

You have completed the questionnaire. Thank you very much for your time and dedication.

Q.29. What's the reason why you don't use electronic resource?

☐ Not aware of electronic resource
☐ Don't know how to use it
☐ Don't need it
☐ Time consuming
☐ Can't access the electronic resource
☐ Others, please specify:_____

You have completed the questionnaire. Thank you very much for your time and dedication.

Appendix B
Inviting Letter

Dear Sir/Madam,

I am currently a PhD student in the School of Business Information Technology, Business Portfolio, RMIT University. My thesis topic is the role of information communication technology in knowledge management. As part of my PhD project, I am investigating the use of electronic resources in library from knowledge management perspective. My supervisors are Dr. Hepu Deng and Prof. Bill Martin, School of Business Information Technology, Business Portfolio, RMIT University.

I am inviting you to participate in an online survey, which takes around 10 to 15 minutes to complete. You just click http://www.rmit.edu.au/bus/bit/e-resources, answer the questions and click 'submit' button to submit your answers. Your participation is completely voluntary and you may withdraw at anytime. This survey is designed to identify the factors influencing the effective use of electronic resources within the context of knowledge management. Your response will be very valuable for the success of this research project and help achieve maximum potential of using electronic resources.

This project is subject to the Ethics Policy and Procedures of RMIT University. We guarantee that all information provided will be treated in complete confidence and that no individual or organisation will be identified. You are free to withdraw from the project at any time and to withdraw any unprocessed data. The data collected will be analyzed and the results are likely to be published in academic journals or presented at academic conferences in the near future.

If you have any queries regarding this project please contact my senior supervisor, Dr. Hepu Deng phone (03) 9925 5823, email hepu.deng@rmit.edu.au, or my second supervisor, Prof. Bill Martin phone (03) 9925 5783, email bill.martin@rmit.edu.au or Prof. Tim Fry, the Chair of the Business Portfolio Human Research Ethics Sub-committee, phone (03) 9925 5594, email rdu@rmit.edu.au.

Thank you very much for your support of my research project.

Yours faithfully,
Hongli Song

Appendix C
A Summary of Crosstabulation Analysis

Table C.1   **A crosstabulation analysis between users' position and usefulness**

		Usefulness					Total
		Extremely useful	**Quite useful**	**Useful**	**Not sure**	**Not useful**	
Academic Staff	Count	31	8	1	0	0	40
	% within group	77.5%	20.0%	2.5%	0.0%	0.0%	100.0%
	% within Usefulness	18.5%	8.2%	5.0%	0.0%	0.0%	13.7%
Administrative Staff	Count	17	8	1	0	0	26
	% within group	65.4%	30.8%	3.8%	0.0%	0.0%	100.0%
	% within Usefulness	10.1%	8.2%	5.0%	0.0%	0.0%	8.9%
Postgraduate Student by Research	Count	37	10	3	0	0	50
	% within group	74.0%	20.0%	6.0%	0.0%	0.0%	100.0%
	% within Usefulness	22.0%	10.3%	15.0%	0.0%	0.0%	17.1%
Postgraduate Student by Coursework	Count	40	19	2	1	0	62
	% within group	64.5%	30.6%	3.2%	1.6%	0.0%	100.0%
	% within Usefulness	23.8%	19.6%	10.0%	16.7%	0.0%	21.2%
Undergraduate &TAFE Student	Count	43	52	13	5	2	115
	% within group	37.4%	45.2%	11.3%	4.3%	1.7%	100.0%
	% within Usefulness	25.6%	53.6%	65.0%	83.3%	100.0%	39.2%
Total	Count	168	97	20	6	2	293
	% within group	57.3%	33.1%	6.8%	2.0%	0.7%	100.0%
	% within Usefulness	100%	100.0%	100.0%	100.0%	100.0%	100.0%

Table C.2   A crosstabulation analysis between users' seniority and usefulness

		Usefulness					Total
		Extremely useful	**Quite useful**	**Useful**	**Not sure**	**Not useful**	
Less than 1 year	Count	46	36	12	4	1	99
	% within group	46.5%	36.4%	12.1%	4.0%	1.0%	100.0%
	% within Usefulness	27.4%	37.1%	60.0%	66.7%	50.0%	33.8%
1-4 years	Count	90	44	6	2	1	143
	% within group	62.9%	30.8%	4.2%	1.4%	0.7%	100.0%
	% within Usefulness	53.6%	45.4%	30.0%	33.3%	50.0%	48.8%
5-10 years	Count	20	13	2	0	0	35
	% within group	57.1%	37.1%	5.7%	0.0%	0.0%	100.0%
	% within Usefulness	11.9%	13.4%	10.0%	0.0%	0.0%	11.9%
11-25 years	Count	8	4	0	0	0	12
	% within group	66.7%	33.3%	0.0%	0.0%	0.0%	100.0%
	% within Usefulness	4.8%	4.1%	0.0%	0.0%	0.0%	4.1%
More than 25 years	Count	4	0	0	0	0	4
	% within group	100.0%	0.0%	0.0%	0.0%	0.0%	100.0%
	% within Usefulness	2.4%	0.0%	0.0%	0.0%	0.0%	1.4%
Total	Count	168	97	20	6	2	293
	% within group	57.3%	33.1%	6.8%	2.0%	0.7%	100.0%
	% within Usefulness	100%	100.0%	100.0%	100.0%	100.0%	100.0%
5 years and more than 5 years	Count	28	17	2	0	0	47
	% within seniority	59.6%	36.2%	4.3%	0.0%	0.0%	100.0%
	% within Usefulness	17.1%	17.5%	10.0%	0.0%	0.0%	16.3%

Table C.3   A crosstabulation analysis between users' age and usefulness

		Usefulness Extremely useful	Quite useful	Useful	Not sure	Not useful	Total
<20	Count	13	22	6	2	1	44
	% within group	29.5%	50.0%	13.6%	4.5%	2.3%	100.0%
	% within Usefulness	7.7%	22.7%	30.0%	33.3%	50.0%	15.0%
20-29	Count	55	39	9	2	1	106
	% within group	51.9%	36.8%	8.5%	1.9%	0.9%	100.0%
	% within Usefulness	32.7%	40.2%	45.0%	33.3%	50.0%	36.2%
30-39	Count	44	17	2	2	0	65
	% within group	67.7%	26.2%	3.1%	3.1%	0.0%	100.0%
	% within Usefulness	26.2%	17.5%	10.0%	33.3%	0.0%	22.2%
40-49	Count	26	12	1	0	0	39
	% within group	66.7%	30.8%	2.6%	0.0%	0.0%	100.0%
	% within Usefulness	15.5%	12.4%	5.0%	0.0%	0.0%	13.3%
50-59	Count	27	5	2	0	0	34
	% within group	79.4%	14.7%	5.9%	0.0%	0.0%	100.0%
	% within Usefulness	16.1%	5.2%	10.0%	0.0%	0.0%	11.6%
>60	Count	3	2	0	0	0	5
	% within group	60.0%	40.0%	0.0%	0.0%	0.0%	100.0%
	% within Usefulness	1.8%	2.1%	0.0%	0.0%	0.0%	1.7%
Total	Count	168	97	20	6	2	293
	% within group	57.3%	33.1%	6.8%	2.0%	0.7%	100.0%
	% within Usefulness	100%	100.0%	100.0%	100.0%	100.0%	100.0%
<30	Count	68	61	15	4	2	150
	% within group	45.3%	40.7%	10.0%	2.7%	1.3%	100.0%
	% within Usefulness	40.5%	62.9%	75.0%	66.7%	100.0%	51.2%
>=30	Count	100	36	5	2	0	143
	% within group	69.9%	25.2%	3.5%	1.4%	0.0%	100.0%
	% within Usefulness	59.5%	37.1%	25.0%	33.3%	0.0%	48.8%

Table C.4   A crosstabulation analysis between users' education and usefulness

		Usefulness					Total
		Extremely useful	Quite useful	Useful	Not sure	Not useful	
PhD or equivalent	Count	18	6	0	0	0	24
	% within group	75.0%	25.0%	0.0%	0.0%	0.0%	100.0%
	% within Usefulness	10.7%	6.2%	0.0%	0.0%	0.0%	8.2%
Postgraduate	Count	58	16	4	0	0	78
	% within group	74.4%	20.5%	5.1%	0.0%	0.0%	100.0%
	% within Usefulness	34.5%	16.5%	20.0%	0.0%	0.0%	26.6%
Undergraduate	Count	54	44	6	5	0	109
	% within group	49.5%	40.4%	5.5%	4.6%	0.0%	100.0%
	% within Usefulness	32.1%	45.4%	30.0%	83.3%	0.0%	37.2%
TAFE	Count	21	17	6	0	0	44
	% within group	47.7%	38.6%	13.6%	0.0%	0.0%	100.0%
	% within Usefulness	12.5%	17.5%	30.0%	0.0%	0.0%	15.0%
High school	Count	17	14	4	1	2	38
	% within group	44.7%	36.8%	10.5%	2.6%	5.3%	100.0%
	% within Usefulness	10.1%	14.4%	20.0%	16.7%	100.0%	13.0%
Total	Count	168	97	20	6	2	293
	% within group	57.3%	33.1%	6.8%	2.0%	0.7%	100.0%
	% within Usefulness	100%	100.0%	100.0%	100.0%	100.0%	100.0%

Table C.5   A crosstabulation analysis between users' gender and usefulness

		Usefulness					Total
		Extremely useful	Quite useful	Useful	Not sure	Not useful	
Female	Count	95	54	11	3	1	164
	% within group	57.9%	32.9%	6.7%	1.8%	0.6%	100.0%
	% within Usefulness	56.5%	55.7%	55.0%	50.0%	50.0%	56.0%
Male	Count	73	43	9	3	1	129
	% within group	56.6%	33.3%	7.0%	2.3%	0.8%	100.0%
	% within Usefulness	43.5%	44.3%	45.0%	50.0%	50.0%	44.0%
Total	Count	168	97	20	6	2	293
	% within group	57.3%	33.1%	6.8%	2.0%	0.7%	100.0%
	% within Usefulness	100%	100.0%	100.0%	100.0%	100.0%	100.0%

Table C. 6   A crosstabulation analysis between part of work/study and usefulness

Part of work/study		Usefulness					Total
		Extremely useful	Quite useful	Useful	Not sure	Not useful	
Missing value	Count	1	0	0	0	0	1
	% within group	100.0%	0.0%	0.0%	0.0%	0.0%	100.0%
	% within Usefulness	0.6%	0.0%	0.0%	0.0%	0.0%	0.3%
Intend to	Count	0	1	2	1	0	4
	% within group	0.0%	25.0%	50.0%	25.0%	0.0%	100.0%
	% within Usefulness	0.0%	1.0%	10.0%	16.7%	0.0%	1.4%
No	Count	7	8	3	1	1	20
	% within group	35.0%	40.0%	15.0%	5.0%	5.0%	100.0%
	% within Usefulness	4.2%	8.2%	15.0%	16.7%	50.0%	6.8%
Yes	Count	160	88	15	4	1	268
	% within group	59.7%	32.8%	5.6%	1.5%	0.4%	100.0%
	% within Usefulness	95.2%	90.7%	75.0%	66.7%	50.0%	91.5%
Total	Count	168	97	20	6	2	293
	% within group	57.3%	33.1%	6.8%	2.0%	0.7%	100.0%
	% within Usefulness	100%	100.0%	100.0%	100.0%	100.0%	100.0%

Table C. 7   A crosstabulation analysis between the integration and usefulness

Integration with tasks		Usefulness					Total
		Extremely useful	Quite useful	Useful	Not sure	Not useful	
Missing value	Count	1	1	0	0	0	2
	% within group	50.0%	50.0%	0.0%	0.0%	0.0%	100.0%
	% within Usefulness	0.6%	1.0%	0.0%	0.0%	0.0%	0.7%
Intend to	Count	8	6	3	1	0	18
	% within group	44.4%	33.3%	16.7%	5.6%	0.0%	100.0%
	% within Usefulness	4.8%	6.2%	15.0%	16.7%	0.0%	6.1%
No	Count	18	27	7	3	2	57
	% within group	31.6%	47.4%	12.3%	5.3%	3.5%	100.0%
	% within Usefulness	10.7%	27.8%	35.0%	50.0%	100.0%	19.5%
Yes	Count	141	63	10	2	0	216
	% within group	65.3%	29.2%	4.6%	0.9%	0.0%	100.0%
	% within Usefulness	83.9%	64.9%	50.0%	33.3%	0.0%	73.7%
Total	Count	168	97	20	6	2	293
	% within group	57.3%	33.1%	6.8%	2.0%	0.7%	100.0%
	% within Usefulness	100%	100.0%	100.0%	100.0%	100.0%	100.0%

Table C. 8   A crosstabulation analysis between express electronically and usefulness

Make ideas available electronically		Usefulness					Total
		Extremely useful	**Quite useful**	**Useful**	**Not sure**	**Not useful**	
Missing value	Count	2	0	0	0	0	2
	% within group	100.0%	0.0%	0.0%	0.0%	0.0%	100.0%
	% within Usefulness	1.2%	0.0%	0.0%	0.0%	0.0%	0.7%
Intend to	Count	16	14	2	1	0	33
	% within group	48.5%	42.4%	6.1%	3.0%	0.0%	100.0%
	% within Usefulness	9.5%	14.4%	10.0%	16.7%	0.0%	11.3%
No	Count	55	54	9	4	2	124
	% within group	44.4%	43.5%	7.3%	3.2%	1.6%	100.0%
	% within Usefulness	32.7%	55.7%	45.0%	66.7%	100.0%	42.3%
Yes	Count	95	29	9	1	0	134
	% within group	70.9%	21.6%	6.7%	0.7%	0.0%	100.0%
	% within Usefulness	56.5%	29.9%	45.0%	16.7%	0.0%	45.7%
Total	Count	168	97	20	6	2	293
	% within group	57.3%	33.1%	6.8%	2.0%	0.7%	100.0%
	% within Usefulness	100%	100.0%	100.0%	100.0%	100.0%	100.0%

Table C. 9   A crosstabulation analysis between publish electronically and usefulness

Publish electronically		Usefulness					Total
		Extremely useful	Quite useful	Useful	Not sure	Not useful	
Intend to	Count	22	6	1	1	0	30
	% within group	73.3%	20.0%	3.3%	3.3%	0.0%	100.0%
	% within Usefulness	13.1%	6.2%	5.0%	16.7%	0.0%	10.2%
No	Count	100	79	18	4	2	203
	% within group	49.3%	38.9%	8.9%	2.0%	1.0%	100.0%
	% within Usefulness	59.5%	81.4%	90.0%	66.7%	100.0%	69.3%
Yes	Count	46	12	1	1	0	60
	% within group	76.7%	20.0%	1.7%	1.7%	0.0%	100.0%
	% within Usefulness	27.4%	12.4%	5.0%	16.7%	0.0%	20.5%
Total	Count	168	97	20	6	2	293
	% within group	57.3%	33.1%	6.8%	2.0%	0.7%	100.0%
	% within Usefulness	100%	100.0%	100.0%	100.0%	100.0%	100.0%

Table C.10   A crosstabulation analysis between users' position and usefulness

(by merging some cells)

		Usefulness		Total
		Extremely useful	**Not extremely useful**	**Total**
Academic Staff	Count	31	9	40
	% within group	77.5%	22.5%	100.0%
	% within Usefulness	18.5%	7.2%	13.7%
Administrative Staff	Count	17	9	26
	% within group	65.4%	34.6%	100.0%
	% within Usefulness	10.1%	7.2%	8.9%
Postgraduate Student by Research	Count	37	13	50
	% within group	74.0%	26.0%	100.0%
	% within Usefulness	22.0%	10.4%	17.1%
Postgraduate Student by Coursework	Count	40	22	62
	% within group	64.5%	35.5%	100.0%
	% within Usefulness	23.8%	17.6%	21.2%
Undergraduate &TAFE Student	Count	43	72	115
	% within group	37.4%	62.6%	100.0%
	% within Usefulness	25.6%	57.6%	39.2%
Total	Count	168	125	293
	% within group	57.3%	42.7%	100.0%
	% within Usefulness	100%	100.0%	100.0%

Table C.11   **A crosstabulation analysis between users' seniority and usefulness**

(by merging some cells)

		Usefulness		Total
		Extremely useful	**Not extremely useful**	**Total**
Less than 1 year	Count	46	53	99
	% within group	46.5%	53.5%	100.0%
	% within Usefulness	27.4%	42.4%	33.8%
1-4 years	Count	90	53	143
	% within group	62.9%	37.1%	100.0%
	% within Usefulness	53.6%	42.4%	48.8%
5 years and more than 5 years	Count	32	19	35
	% within group	62.7%	37.3%	100.0%
	% within Usefulness	19.0%	15.2%	11.9%
Total	Count	168	125	293
	% within group	57.3%	42.7%	100.0%
	% within Usefulness	100.0%	100.0%	100.0%

Table C.12   **A crosstabulation analysis between users' age and usefulness**

(by merging some cells)

		Usefulness			Total
		Extremely useful	**Quite useful**	**Useful Not sure Not useful**	**Total**
<30	Count	68	61	21	44
	% within group	45.3%	40.7%	14.0%	100.0%
	% within Usefulness	40.5%	62.9%	75.0%	15.0%
>=30	Count	100	36	7	106
	% within group	69.9%	25.2%	4.9%	100.0%
	% within Usefulness	59.5%	37.1%	25.0%	36.2%
Total	Count	168	97	28	293
	% within group	57.3%	33.1%	9.6%	100.0%
	% within Usefulness	100.0%	100.0%	100.0%	100.0%

Table C.13   A crosstabulation analysis between users' education and usefulness

(by merging some cells)

| | | Usefulness | | Total |
		Extremely useful	Not extremely useful	
PhD or equivalent	Count	18	6	24
	% within group	75.0%	25.0%	100.0%
	% within Usefulness	10.7%	4.8%	8.2%
Postgraduate	Count	58	20	78
	% within group	74.4%	25.6%	100.0%
	% within Usefulness	34.5%	16.0%	26.6%
Undergraduate	Count	54	55	109
	% within group	49.5%	50.5%	100.0%
	% within Usefulness	32.1%	44.0%	37.2%
TAFE	Count	21	23	44
	% within group	47.7%	52.3%	100.0%
	% within Usefulness	12.5%	18.4%	15.0%
High school	Count	17	21	38
	% within group	44.7%	55.3%	100.0%
	% within Usefulness	10.1%	16.8%	13.0%
Total	Count	168	125	293
	% within group	57.3%	42.7%	100.0%
	% within Usefulness	100.0%	100.0%	100.0%

Table C.14   A crosstabulation analysis between users' gender and usefulness

(by merging some cells)

		Usefulness			Total
		Extremely useful	Quite useful	Useful Not sure Not useful	
Female	Count	95	54	15	164
	% within group	57.9%	32.9%	9.1%	100.0%
	% within Usefulness	56.5%	55.7%	53.6%	56.0%
Male	Count	73	43	13	129
	% within group	56.6%	33.3%	10.1%	100.0%
	% within Usefulness	43.5%	44.3%	46.4%	44.0%
Total	Count	168	97	28	293
	% within group	57.3%	33.1%	9.6%	100.0%
	% within Usefulness	100.0%	100.0%	100.0%	100.0%

Table C. 15   A crosstabulation analysis between part of work/study and usefulness

(by merging some cells)

Part of work/study		Usefulness			Total
		Extremely useful	Quite useful	Useful Not sure Not useful	
Intend to or No	Count	7	9	8	24
	% within group	29.2%	37.5%	33.3%	100.0%
	% within Usefulness	4.2%	9.3%	28.6%	8.2%
Yes	Count	160	88	20	268
	% within group	59.7%	32.8%	7.5%	100.0%
	% within Usefulness	95.8%	90.7%	71.4%	91.8%
Total	Count	167	97	28	292
	% within group	57.2%	33.2%	9.6%	100.0%
	% within Usefulness	100.0%	100.0%	100.0%	100.0%

Table C. 16   A crosstabulation analysis between the integration and usefulness

(by merging some cells)

Integration with tasks		Usefulness			Total
		Extremely useful	**Quite useful**	**Useful Not sure Not useful**	**Total**
Missing value	Count	1	1	0	2
	% within group	50.0%	50.0%	0.0%	100.0%
	% within Usefulness	0.6%	1.0%	0.0%	0.7%
Intend to or No	Count	26	33	16	75
	% within group	34.7%	44.0%	21.3%	100.0%
	% within Usefulness	15.6%	34.4%	57.1%	25.8%
Yes	Count	141	63	12	216
	% within group	65.3%	29.2%	5.6%	100.0%
	% within Usefulness	84.4%	65.6%	42.9%	73.7%
Total	Count	168	97	28	293
	% within group	57.3%	33.1%	9.6%	100.0%
	% within Usefulness	100%	100.0%	100.0%	100.0%

Table C. 17   A crosstabulation analysis between express electronically and usefulness

(by merging some cells)

Make ideas available electronically		Usefulness			Total
		Extremely useful	Quite useful	Useful Not sure Not useful	
Missing value	Count	2	0	0	2
	% within group	100.0%	0.0%	0.0%	100.0%
	% within Usefulness	1.2%	0.0%	0.0%	0.7%
Intend to or No	Count	71	68	18	157
	% within group	45.2%	43.3%	11.5%	100.0%
	% within Usefulness	42.8%	70.1%	64.3%	54.0%
Yes	Count	95	29	10	134
	% within group	70.9%	21.6%	7.5%	100.0%
	% within Usefulness	57.2%	29.9%	35.7%	45.7%
Total	Count	168	97	28	293
	% within group	57.3%	33.3%	9.6%	100.0%
	% within Usefulness	100%	100.0%	100.0%	100.0%

Table C. 18   A crosstabulation analysis between publish electronically and usefulness

(by merging some cells)

Publish electronically		Usefulness		Total
		Extremely useful	**Not extremely useful**	
Intend to or No	Count	122	111	233
	% within group	52.4%	47.6%	100.0%
	% within Usefulness	72.6%	88.8%	79.5%
Yes	Count	46	14	60
	% within group	76.7%	23.3%	100.0%
	% within Usefulness	27.4%	11.2%	20.5%
Total	Count	168	97	293
	% within group	57.3%	33.1%	100.0%
	% within Usefulness	100%	100.0%	100.0%

Appendix D
Interview Questions

Section A: background questions (to all interviewees)

1. What is your current position?
2. How long have you been working in the current institution and position?
3. What are the main scope and responsibilities of your position?
4. Are you part of knowledge portal project members?
5. Have you ever used the knowledge portal?

Section B: implementation issues (to knowledge portal project team members)

1. what drove the knowledge portal initiative?
2. how did the project start and proceed?
3. what's the plan to implement the knowledge portal?
4. why did you select the technology/tools to achieve the objectives?
5. how did you select the technology/tools to achieve the objectives?
6. how much is the budget for the project?
7. how did you get the budget?
8. what is the current implementation status of the knowledge portal project?
9. what do you think of the usefulness for knowledge portal functionalities?
10. how would you describe the overall attitude of the people involved towards knowledge portal project?
11. what problems have you encountered in implementing knowledge portal and how severe is each problem?

12. what factors facilitated and prohibited the implementation of the knowledge portal?

13. how do you assess the success of the project?

Section C: consequences (to inside-users)

1. what's your expectation before you used the knowledge portal?
2. what's your experience after you used the knowledge portal?
3. will you stop your previous practice and change to use the knowledge portal?
4. what are reasons why you want to change to use the knowledge portal?

Section D: consequences (to non-users)

1. What are reasons why you have not used the knowledge portal?
2. What is your own practice to do the same task with knowledge portal?
3. What are the disadvantages and advantages to keep your own practice?

Section E: consequences (to outside-users)

1. why are you interested in the knowledge portal?
2. what's disadvantages and advantages to re-use the knowledge portal framework for your institution?
3. what do you change to suit your institution and why?
4. what factors do you encounter to impact the implementing the knowledge portal in your institution?

Appendix E

Plain Language Statement

10 September 2005

Dear Participant,

I am currently a PhD student in the School of Business Information Technology at RMIT Business. My thesis topic is the role of information communication technology in knowledge management and my supervisors are Dr. Hepu Deng and Prof. Bill Martin.

This interview is part of my research project and it aims to enlist your experience, opinion, attitude and perception about the use of knowledge portal for program quality management. Your response will be very valuable for the success of the implementation of the knowledge portal and help improve program quality management.

I am inviting you to participate in my research. Your participation will involve an interview, which takes around 30 to 60 minutes to complete. Participation in this research is voluntary and you may withdraw at anytime.

The data collected will be analysed for my thesis and the results may appear in publications. The results will be reported in a manner which does not enable you to be identified. Thus the reporting will protect your anonymity.

If you have any queries regarding this project please contact my senior supervisor, Dr. Hepu Deng phone (03) 9925 5823, email hepu.deng@rmit.edu.au, or my second supervisor, Prof. Bill Martin phone (03) 9925 5783, email bill.martin@rmit.edu.au or the Business Portfolio Human Research Ethics Sub-committee, phone (03) 9925 5594, email rdu@rmit.edu.au.

Yours sincerely,

Hongli Song

Appendix F
List of Tables

Appendix G
List of Figures